Conflict

how it starts / how to stop it

Also by Micheal Lawson for Christian Focus
God's Master Plan

CONFLICT

Michael Lawson

Christian Focus

ISBN 1 857 925 289

Copyright © Michael Lawson

This edition published by Christian Focus Publications in 1999. First published in Great Britian in 1991 by Hodder and Stoughton. All rights reserved. No part of this publication may be reproduced or transmitted in any form or by any means, electronic or mechinal, including photocopying, recording, or any information storage or retrieval system, without either prior permission in writing from the publisher or a licence permitting restricted copying.

CONTENTS

How to use this book 7

PART ONE THE ROOTS OF CONFLICT
1 The part we play 13
2 Our powerful past 33
3 The way we see things 57

PART TWO INTERPERSONAL CONFLICT
4 Family relationships 81
5 Work relationships 103
6 Marriage relationships 123

PART THREE INNER CONFLICT
7 Conflicts of spirit 153

PART FOUR RESOLVING CONFLICT
8 New ways to respond 175
9 New attitudes to learn 197

HOW TO USE THIS BOOK

This is a book about people and what happens when they don't get on. It's a *self-help* book, designed to enable you to manage better the conflicts and strained relationships in your life, or the life of someone close to you. Conflict is a wide-ranging and comprehensive subject. Not everyone faces the same kinds of conflict. The treatment of such a subject therefore risks potentially encyclopaedic dimensions: to cover every kind of conflict, experienced by every kind of person, in every kind of situation!

This is not an omnibus, though many familiar situations of conflict are covered and fully explored. It is, however, my conviction that there are *common factors* in all the varied conflicts we may experience and the part we may play in them. Equally, there are *common principles* which positively apply to the constructive approach, we can learn to contribute both to resolving and preventing conflict, no matter what the situation may be.

If, therefore, you have picked up this book hoping to find quick solutions to problems, I hope you will be challenged rather than disappointed. No matter what the conflict or the circumstances you may be facing, the principles of human conduct and response remain the same. The guidelines you will find here will help you face issues both within yourself and with others. The pen and paper exercises, and the thinking-points, are designed not only to stimulate but to help you grapple with important issues which affect you as a person. The approach is eclectic, based on Biblical understanding and insights from counselling theory and psychology. All truth is God's truth, and its careful, thorough application liberates in practice.

Part One, on the roots of conflict, is about the important part *we* play. It helps us see within ourselves the elements which we contribute to conflict situations. These three chapters aim to help promote insight, understanding and personal growth in the area of attitudes, personality and the part played by our past and early upbringing. This section lays the groundwork. It should not be missed.

Part Two, on interpersonal conflict, examines three areas of conflict most commonly experienced: family, work, and marriage relationships. All three chapters contain important principles for the areas of experience concerned, and give Biblical perspectives on the dynamics of these relationships. They will be of greatest interest to those whose lives are affected in these ways.

Part Three, on inner conflict, looks at conflicts of the spirit. Not all conflicts involve other people. We are often battling within ourselves. We may experience striving, temptation, bewilderment and soul searching. At the deepest level, much of the dis-ease we feel is spiritual in origin and essence. It is with that awareness that the searching issues of desire and covetousness are fully examined. This is set in the context of spiritual realism: the struggle we have with knowing and obeying the will of God.

Part Four, on resolving conflict, deals with new ways to respond and new attitudes to learn. The skills of interpersonal behaviour, particularly listening and verbal skills, are thoroughly examined. Attitudes to anxiety, fear, bitterness, hate and forgiveness are dealt with Biblically and practically.

My training and experience in counselling, both secular and Christian, have brought me in contact with practically every kind of conflict situation faced by individuals from all walks of life. From many hours of talking and working with those in such difficulties, a clear conviction has emerged in my approach to such issues. From the conflicts I have observed in others (and the conflicts I have known myself) I am convinced it is only by facing the issues *underlying* those conflicts that real and lasting progress can be made.

It has been a privilege over the years to see many people take hold of the principles in this book, and emerge from conflict situations, wiser, happier, and above all more in tune with their relationships with others and with God. It is for this reason that I have used actual case histories to illustrate the practical outworkings of real-life conflicts. I have, however, in each case changed names and details; in no way is it possible to perceive the identity of any person here described, either living or dead. The real experiences of others, though disguised, nonetheless provide a tangible way of helping readers identify with the pain and struggle which so many experience and, most importantly, with their potential resolution.

It is my sincerest prayer that as you read these pages God will enable you to find new understanding, insight and strength to face and overcome the issues of conflict in your life and others. Conflict need not be a foe. Of course there are many situations in our lives which can be deeply hurtful, upsetting and destructive. But Christians believe in a God who can transform lives and relationships and make all things new. And new routes for coping with conflict, following the ways of God, can bring long-hoped-for resolution to tired and stressed relationships, and a refreshed joy in living. May your journey of renewed understanding be profoundly beneficial.

Michael Lawson

Part One

The Roots of Conflict

1
THE PART WE PLAY

No one escapes conflict. The nicest and the nastiest all suffer from it. However wise and fairminded we are, anyone can suddenly find themselves in a fight for which they've never bargained.

You drive on to a roundabout, another driver smashes right into your rear, you are determined to remain calm. He hit you, no point in making a meal out of it. But before you know it, you're right in there hammer and tongs, defending yourself against an onslaught of outrage and invective.

There's no immunity from conflict. It gets us all in the end. Its targets are wide, its pains prolonged. Arguments, aggression, even complete relationship breakdowns can happen to anyone. Regardless of the deftness we normally bring to our relationships, when conflict surfaces its power to overwhelm us can be deeply perplexing.

Yet what is conflict in its essence? It's easy to recognise its surface symptoms: the anger, the panic, the shakes and the collywobbles. None of us welcomes the unpleasant responses it stimulates. But the working basis of conflict is confrontation, a clash of interests, an argument, perhaps an ongoing state of active and continuous dissatisfaction. Its effects are both personal and global, touching the lives of individuals, families, whole organisations, even nations or groups of nations. Conflict begins with matters of value, concern, action or philosophy. It can end with agitation, anger, hostile action, even the termination of otherwise long-cherished human bonds of friendship and marriage.

Heated tempers

George and Helen have been married forty-five years. They are not the sort you'd expect to quarrel, at least not violently. Yet quarrel they did after George's retirement. Helen used to have the house to herself. Suddenly her preserve has been violated.

'This is my house, too, you know, Helen. If I want to move the television, I've got a perfect right to do so. Anyway, I paid for the blessed thing.'

'Well, George, if we are going to start arguing that way, who provided the money for the deposit on this house in the first place?'

'Come off it, Helen, that was forty years ago. I'm the one who's sacrificed my life paying for the house and its repairs and its decoration, and all the rest of it . . . '

And so it went on, neither of them hearing the real concern of the other. Each of them getting more heated by the blow. Until there was a sudden crash. Helen swears it was an accident. They told the insurance company the same. The insurance men quite often have claims like that: a damaged television, injured by a flying flower vase!

Whose fault?

Conflict can take place anywhere. It happens out on the streets, behind closed doors, in corridors of power, in the seat of government. Wherever it is, who's to blame? Whose *fault* is conflict? Of course, it takes two to make an argument. So there's always a role for someone else, active or passive. Only inner conflicts fly solo. Disputations don't come without sparring partners. And when the sparring hots up, the blow can sting. The effects of verbal abuse can be shattering.

Conflict, then, is at best uncomfortable, at worst highly destructive. Whatever its form, most of us would never court it. The hurt, the fear, the affront, the sheer injustice of it all; if we do not run away altogether, we inwardly shrink from it.

Often those on the outside calmly suggest, 'Why don't you talk it out, quietly and urbanely?' If only we could. Trouble is, we get caught off guard. We are confronted and we confront back. We switch on to autopilot. Emotions quickly bubble to the surface. The waters get muddied. Whatever happened to my quiet life? Before we know it, we are facing conflict . . .

Of course, there are factors within our conflicts with others that affect the purely *external* circumstances of our lives. The neighbour who wants to block out my light by building his new garage, or the teenage son who treats my home like a hotel – all may spoil my day, negatively affecting the way I choose to conduct my life. But these practical issues aside, there is a more subtle dimension to conflict which is almost always at work when interpersonal disagreements arise.

My role

When conflict does occur it's always *their* fault, isn't it? My personal reaction may often be to see the problem originating with the attitudes, beliefs, or actions of the *other* person. In fact, a most significant area for dealing with the problem, if not in some cases accounting for it altogether, is to realise a major part lies not outside ourselves (in them and their attitudes), but with me (in me and my attitudes – in my inner reactions, habits of mind, prejudices and habitual behaviour given certain threatening circumstances). The person who has just sent me into an inner panic of humiliated pride, anger and singeing hurt may have less responsibility in the matter than I may be inclined to attribute to them. Maybe I feel like throwing something in their direction, physically, verbally, or just under my breath. They may have behaved badly, rudely, aggressively, even unforgivably. But what is *my* role in all this? That's the question we all have to ask, and keep on asking. *What part am I playing in the conflict process?*

The growth process

Conflict doesn't just happen, it has its own process of growth. Anyone who has forgotten to take a glass bottle out of the freezer will know the shattering consequence. But it takes quite a time for the liquid to solidify and the glass to splinter and fragment. It's the same with conflict. Conflict is a dynamic process; and its destructive and long-term effects depend upon a number of factors, not least of which is the inner you, the real person beneath the surface. That is you with all your qualities, sensitivities and weaknesses; you with all your experience of growing up, living and growing older; you with all your joys and aspirations, as well as (like us all) your strong sense of individual identity and pride.

No doubles

As a human being, made in the image of God, you are unique. There's no one quite like you. They say we all have our double, and it can be fascinating and sometimes puzzling by chance to see someone on TV, in the paper, or in the street who looks in every sense your mirror image, your stand-in should you ever become a star of stage and film. But when it comes to our emotional profile, to our below-surface identity, then there are no longer any doubles. You are the only candidate for the role, since so much, remembered and unremembered, has made you what you are. The catalogue of personal influence which has lent you your unique inner identity is simply enormous.

The personality response

What you are under the surface plays an important part in how you respond to a variety of human circumstances. There are many examples. We all have different likes and dislikes, different tastes in food, music, films and clothes. We may like or dislike different activities with particularly strong feelings involved. Some men are mad keen on football. Others can't stand the game. Some women love dressmaking or knitting. Others hate the very thought of them.

These simple levels of personality illustrate a significant element. Likes and dislikes cannot be put down to pure genetic inheritance alone. We are not pre-programmed machines, though we all carry with us important biological inheritances which as much affect the colour of our eyes as our purely human gifts and abilities. Many of our basic likes and dislikes probably have some explanation in the long chain of experience, if only we could piece the jigsaw together.

There was some laughter at a dinner party when one of the guests admitted she had eaten and enjoyed a plate of spinach for the first time in twenty-five years. As a youngster she had detested the Popeye cartoons on television. She'd firmly resisted her mother's oft-repeated efforts to tempt her with the power-packed vegetable which she'd seen the singing sailor-man so often greedily guzzle straight from the can. Not until her mid-thirties did she find her taste change, and even then by chance, as good manners constrained her to eat what she had for so many years quite strenuously resisted. We have all inherited personal preferences in one shape or form by a variety of different roots; some of those origins are clear, others of them are lost in the entanglements of time and circumstance.

Likes and dislikes apart, the inheritance which matters most for our thinking at this stage is more to do with what has fashioned our inner responses, especially the responses which cause us discomfort, anger, anxiety or conflict.

Fire down below

Suppose someone you know has recently accused you of an uncaring hypocritical attitude. You're not sure why this criticism comes so vigorously your way. What you do know is that it has caused you considerable hurt and pain. Perhaps you're not a person to take criticism lying down and you have had some sharp exchanges with your friend. You may not have behaved too badly under the circumstances (though we all have a limit to the length of our inner fuse); but how much of the conflict was contributed by the part of you over which you seem to have less control, the fire down below, the lesser-disciplined arena of your own strong inner responses?

Let's say your friend misinterpreted your motive for acting as you did. You may have cancelled an appointment, disappointing your friend, who now complains loudly and aggressively that you are an uncaring suit-yourself sort, whose commitment to friendship is purely selfish. Maybe he is over-reacting. But is the resulting conflict really all his fault? After all, some people confronted with the same issue might smile quietly and respond gently and constructively until the issue blew over.

Pre-programmed?

Conflict is personal in that it affects different people in different ways. One man's conflict may be water which flows unceremoniously off another's back; no sweat, no hassle. Clearly personal reactions provide important personal clues. Machines we are not, but perhaps after all there are hidden 'pre-programmed' factors within us which are also part of the story, which affect our response to conflict.

Take the broken appointment with your friend. Is it the first time, for instance, you have been told you only enter into relationships for what you can get out of them? When we come to consider the importance of our individual life stories, we'll see more clearly the significance of these echoes from the past. It may hurt to hear accusing comments like this – for highly-charged emotions are often linked to equally-highly-charged events, or a series of events, from our past. These, as we shall see later, can also be tied into all kinds of empowered emotions, such as anger, fear, hate and loathing.

It is a fact that the issues and situations of conflict which most unsettle, pressurise and perplex us have their roots deep within our inner selves. For though conflict arises often from the aggressive attitudes of others, it feeds not so much on this as on the learned and unlearned responses of our inner world. Our responses are triggered and not always *caused* by these confrontations.

Deep wells

Our inner responses to conflict are often dredged up from deep and sometimes murky wells within us. They may be conditioned by behavioural and emotional experiences from our early life and learning.

We can, of course, overdramatise the interior elements in conflict. If someone stupidly backs into my car because they were chatting away to their passenger, I have a right to be cross. I'll soon calm down, and so should they. All the details will be sorted out, and their action may continue to be an irritation until the car is repaired and the claim settled. But the conflict is now over. I hardly need to be too soul-searching to understand my reasonable response.

More deep-seated conflict is by definition more complex to resolve. It is often the *negative* power I perceive within myself that is so difficult to account for, or control. You can be in good shape, mentally, physically and spiritually, yet suddenly find yourself in a situation where destructive power from within seeks to engulf you. You can certainly repress your feelings, but sometimes they simply will not lie down and be forgotten or ignored. You might expect Christians to be the last group of people to be involved in strong confrontations. Yet the New Testament is full of evidence of the squabbling of the early Church. The Christians in the Roman colony at Corinth were notorious for issuing lawsuits just to resolve bitter disputes between one Christian and another (cf. 1 Cor. 6). This made for strong teaching from the Apostle Paul. But it remains a fact that then, as now, even those highly motivated to peaceful living often find that there is a power working against them from within. And self-knowledge at this point is of inestimable value in strengthening oneself against the conflict response.

Everything just so . . .

Julia is an attractive and intelligent woman in her early thirties. She works in a local newspaper office, normally manages well with her work and often tells others how enjoyable she finds it. But recently Julia has been encountering difficulties. Her major problem is to do with two new girls who have just joined as WP operators. They are both in their late teens and they appear to do far less than their fair share of the office load, often leaving important copy work uncompleted at five o'clock, so that Julia has to authorise overtime payments for them.

It seems that Julia's irritated remarks have been heard once too often by Karen and Sarah, and some angry comments have recently been made. 'You want everything to be perfect, Julia. You're always bossing us about. Anyway, you're not so perfect yourself . . .'

THE PART WE PLAY

Such remarks would not be so noteworthy if they had not sent Julia into a frenzy of concern and inward panic. She feels a barrier has gone up between them, that her comments to the girls were perfectly justified and that the whole thing has been thrown back in her face. It has come down to personalities and Julia is very disturbed by it all.

When Julia confided in her husband, his response was carefully considered. Those who are close to us can sometimes possess an objectivity about our makeup which we sometimes fail to perceive ourselves. Without communicating criticism, David was able to convey to Julia something which helped her to see herself through the eyes of others.

'I found it so insulting, David. Anyway, why shouldn't I expect high standards from them? I keep a very high standard. They should too.'

David was quiet in his response, not arguing with Julia as she was still pretty keyed up.

'There's no reason at all why you shouldn't expect good quality work, Julia,' David said calmly. 'But that's you, isn't it? You've grown up that way. Your father always insisted on everything being just so. Didn't you say that he'd expect you to tidy your bedroom every day before you went to school and at night before you went to bed, that everything had to be perfectly in place? I wonder what that did to you, especially the daily nagging and complaining until you got it right.'

Julia's attention was caught.

'You know, Julia, perhaps you sometimes ask too much of those girls. I know they take liberties. But it's your response to them that's really the issue here. Being told in a spiteful, truculent way that you're not perfect rings louder bells for you than it would for most. I'm not surprised you were upset, the resonances go deep, don't they? It makes you feel you are not acceptable as a person . . .'

This caused Julia to pause and think, especially David's final comments on the matter.

'Do you think your dad's attitudes actually left their mark? After all, you make the same unrealistic demands on me sometimes, and I'm not perfect either – only I've never confronted you with the unreasonableness of it all.'

Facing up to self

In any situation of conflict, whether serious or trivial, the complexities of our inner self are likely to be of equal, if not more significance, than the role of the other party. Each individual is responsible for who they are, for what they say and do. We are responsible for our own unique reaction. Any attempt to help us overcome the weakness we may feel when encountering conflict must allow for this fundamental element in conflict management.

At the same time the other party, or parties, involved will have their sensitivities too, and understanding them will be another key to successful conflict management. We'll need to ask what we have contributed to the conflict which elicits the frustrated, rankled response from our friend, colleague, or neighbour. Behaviour which seems innocuous to one person can be a red rag to another. We can all be extremely 'annoying' and not realise it. There will also be deep-seated reasons why certain types of behaviour elicit strong responses in others. These also need attention if we are to live peaceably with those close to us. But self-understanding comes first.

The transformation principle

It would be only too easy to dig up fifty tips for overcoming conflict. We all love short cuts. But serious conflict cannot be managed by way of instant solutions.

Simplified, formula-like techniques are inconsequential when compared with personal growth as a means of overcoming difficulties. It's all very well telling someone to bite their tongue and not fight back. It may be wise and sensible advice given certain circumstances. But it will never deal with the seething frustration which causes you to kick the cat and spend the rest of the evening in a foul and truculent mood. Good tips are fine, but only when the more serious issues are given due attention.

The New Testament never deals in simplified formulas. Its teaching declares that God is concerned for our personal growth and transformation. The quality of our lives is not meant to be static. Far from it. Those who seek to follow Jesus Christ, and in doing so to know the power and purpose of God in their lives, are called to a life of transformation. That transformation comes about by the renewing of our individual minds, a change wrought from the inside, so that all that is weakest, pained and most fragmented within us becomes strengthened and renewed by the truth and love of God (cf. Rom. 12:2). How else can we progress to this high point of the Bible's expectation of sanctified behaviour? 'Bless those who persecute you; bless and do not curse' (Rom. 12:14). That's Biblical conflict management. But to reach that point in our dealings with others a great deal needs to have taken place within us.

This teaching on relationships in Paul's letter to the Romans comes as the climax of a detailed treatise expounding Paul's gospel, the peace which God makes between man and himself. The consequence and outcome of such work enable us to develop relationships of peace with one another. Paul always adds a practical and pastoral application to his theological teaching in his letters. And so his words, 'Bless those who persecute you; bless and do not curse' sound like a counsel of perfection only if we fail to realise the process of transformation which is needed to enable us realistically to respond in this way to aggression from others. For such a response to become our regular practice implies much personal reordering, discipline and growth. The principle Paul is expounding applies to all human differences. For we may not be able to control the behaviour or attitudes of others, *but we can modify our own responses*. For the Christian this will mean entering into a dialogue with God's word as it touches on issues requiring change, which we shall be investigating later.

In situations of conflict, we often have to ask ourselves, 'Why do I find this such a hard situation to manage?' Such a question can be highly revealing. The question may have an obvious answer at a superficial level: anyone might complain loudly when faced with argument, abuse and aggression. Yet conflict may be handled more effectively if what is going on within is taken into account as well as what is going on at the surface.

The worst times of my life

This would be a good point to stop and remind yourself of the kinds of situations and issues which have caused you conflict in the past and may be doing so at present. This conflict inventory could help you to see whether there are any patterns or connections to the concerns you have found most difficult, both past and present. Naturally there will be memories of matters you felt were entirely the fault of others. But even in these situations, is there anything to be learned from your own responses? Keep these findings by you for you'll need them later on. A pencil and paper will be useful as you go through the various exercises in this book.

- What are your worst memories as far as conflict is concerned?
- Is there any kind of conflict which upsets you more than others?
- Can you think of reasons in others which account for the way you react as you do?

- Some people say certain responses in others make them see red and they are guaranteed to be upset, even though for the sake of peace they may repress their anger or hurt. Do you have any reactions like that?
- Can you work out why?
- Do you think you have habits of speech or behaviour, or any regular ways of behaving or responding, which cause others frustration or annoyance?
- If you do, why do you think these cause such irritation?
- Are there any kinds of conflict situation which you strenuously avoid, and why?
- Are there any kinds of conflict situation in which you find yourself often (or even court!) and why?

It may be that I find a situation hard to manage because I am apparently unable to prevent myself from reacting with paralysing anger when spoken to in this way. 'If only I could control my responses, but I seem unable to do anything about them.' Like Julia's situation (p. 20ff), even if the explanation is not as deep-seated as hers, the initial problem lies within myself; something hidden exerts a controlling influence and disables my ability to manage my reactions maturely. It's the ghost in the machine needing to be unmasked and disarmed.

We've already seen that just as we have different tastes, so we all have different sensitivities. Without being over-complicated or analytical, many of our sensitivities are due to early life and subsequent experience. That's why we should now make a start on reminding ourselves of the relevance of our own particular life story.

Identity, self-image and personal history

Who we are now is a mixture of what we let others see of ourselves and what we hide away. Our hidden self may be purposely concealed from the outside world, or something we keep from our own waking mind as too unsettling for conscious thought. The hidden and the unconcealed both belong to history. What we are in all our shapes and sizes has been fashioned and contoured through both inheritance and experience – the comprehensive impact upon us of our parents, childhood and upbringing, and with it those joys, dramas and significant experiences which contribute to what is sometimes called our adult self.

Biography time

How much do you know about yourself? You should be an expert. Surprisingly, many of us know about the events of our lives without always seeing their significance, singly or cumulatively. We are, therefore, going to spend some time getting to know the real you. Conflict cannot be managed effectively unless the conflict manager is fully in possession of his or her own potential contribution to any conflict. So here is an opportunity for 'abbreviated' interpretative biography. It takes far less time than full-scale autobiography, for we are looking for a profile of the significant events that have made you the distinctive person that you are (warts and all, as they say). If you are really concerned to manage conflict better, don't skip this pen and paper exercise. If you wish, you can always read on and come back and do the exercises later.

Start by imagining a meeting between yourself and a total stranger, such as a new family doctor or a church minister. They know nothing about you but, because of their profession, you can completely trust their confidentiality. Your task is to tell them about your life and what makes you the person you are today. Take your time, it is really the highlights they are after. What would you tell them? Imagine yourself making a few notes before the meeting. What would you write down?

THE PART WE PLAY

You may be quite used to talking *about* yourself but you may be less used to *finding connections* in your experience. Whatever your skill:

- Can you say what stands out in your childhood as a positive contribution to your life now?
- Can you say what stands out in your childhood as a negative contribution to your life now?
- Describe one happy childhood memory. Why was it happy?
- What do you consider to be the most formative experiences of your life so far, the painful as well as the good?
- Describe one unhappy childhood memory. Why was it unhappy?
- Can you now describe the kind of person you are as an adult? What words would you use to describe your emotional characteristics? Are you outgoing, shy, optimistic, gloomy, etc? Try and find as many characteristics as possible.
- Are you particularly like any member of your family?
- Emotionally and behaviourally, how do you think you are like or unlike your mother and father? You should answer separately for each of them, or for those who took their place in your childhood.
- What impact, if any, did a brother(s) or sister(s), or being an only child, have upon you?
- Draw two large circles. In the first write all those events and relationships from childhood which seem most significant to you as you think about them now. Use summary phrases. In the second write in those childhood events or aspects of relationships which have most significantly influenced and perhaps continue to influence your *present* experience.
- You could end up by making a picture, abstract or in some way representational, which shows the connections of your childhood to your mature adult life.

This last drawing exercise is a summary of the simple process of thinking which leads us into a deeper appreciation of how we have come to be what we are. Much of how and why we react as we do is based on such factors. There may well have been some particularly sensitive elements in what you have thought about. In particular, when we have been wronged, certain kinds of inner energy responses are set up. These energies often lie dormant till triggered by some unforeseen event or response.

Doreen's Dad

She always called him 'Father' as far back as she could remember. Doreen was brought up abroad. Her father had been a tight-lipped rather unloving man who had apparently taken little interest in Doreen. His marriage to Doreen's mother, who was the epitome of affection and kindness to her only daughter, was a stormy affair. After her mother's untimely death through cancer, Doreen's father returned to England where he put the eight-year-old in the care of an au pair and hardly ever saw her, except to exert some strong-handed discipline when Doreen had done something to displease either the au pair or himself. Yet Doreen's aunt and the au pair, who was quite a caring sort, did much to sweeten the latter part of Doreen's childhood. But, as might be expected, there is some negative legacy from the past in Doreen's adult experience.

Doreen sometimes finds herself in conflict situations which she finds unusually difficult to manage. Typical was the day when she had another disagreement with the headmaster at the local primary school. He simply would not accept that her two children should be allowed any further time off school for the purpose of family holidays. Doreen was convinced he was being unreasonable, but she could not account for her intense feelings of rage. She ended up being very rude to the man.

Doreen knew her anger wouldn't help matters at all. It didn't, and she was shown the door. As she drove back home through the traffic, memories of her father's authoritarian presence, vigorously admonishing her for the sinfulness of some childlike request, filled her mind with pain and loathing. Then came the longing for her mother's warmth and comfort. As it did, a car hooted behind her. The traffic lights were green. Doreen stopped day-dreaming. She'd write that headmaster a strong letter. She'd tell him a few home truths about his condescending, heartless, authoritarian attitude. She'd fight back. It made her feel better.

Know your story

Doreen's story is unique to her. Doreen is not 'neurotic'. Like many, she has her own stock of painful experiences which sometimes affect her present life. Not everything in the past works that way. The fact that as a teenager she had a series of complicated operations for a badly broken leg does not seem to have affected her at all. She tells her children to be careful on the swings, but that's not unusual. We need to beware of thinking a psychoanalyst's couch would give us enough excuses either to blow away all our adult responsibilities, or to explain in detail every feature or peculiarity of our present thoughts or behaviour. It doesn't work like that, for the past is past for most of us.

Nonetheless, the past does exert its moulding influence upon us. Just as a tall building is constructed in layers, so our personalities, emotional characteristics and complexities are built up with the present as the top storey. But there can be shaky elements at any level. There may be issues left unresolved, old hurts or fears. The nearer the foundations, the more likely they are to unsettle or destabilise the whole structure. It is often observed in helping those with complex personal problems that childhood and adolescent experiences are the most important in understanding adult difficulties.

Pause for thought

So what have you discovered about your own story in relation to your experience of conflict? If you haven't yet discovered anything of particular significance (as long as you are sure you have been thorough and answered the questions honestly), don't worry. There's no point in looking for problems when problems don't exist. You will still have been able to describe your emotional characteristics and personality, and that's important in its own right. Most of us should have some clues as to why we are as we are. And it is important to know your own story. We are all sensitive creatures, however we may seem on the outside. In this respect experiences matter far more than appearances.

Let's remember that God wants to help us with our experience of conflict. He wants to provide us with the insight from his word and the power from his Holy Spirit that our lives should be transformed. Dwell for a few moments on these words of Paul, and when you have a moment of quiet use the prayer that follows, either in your own words or as it stands, as a way of bringing to God your thoughts and feelings both on what you have discovered through these pages, and any particular concerns you may have at this present moment.

> Do not grieve the Holy Spirit with whom you were sealed for the day of redemption. Get rid of all bitterness, rage and anger, brawling and slander, along with every form of malice. Be kind and compassionate to one another, forgiving each other, just as in Christ God forgave you. Be imitators of God, therefore, as dearly loved children, and live a life of love, just as Christ loved us and gave himself up

THE PART WE PLAY

for us as a fragrant offering and sacrifice to God (Eph. 4:30–5:2).

Heavenly Father, thank you that as I come to you with my concerns about the conflicts in my life I come to a God who understands my humanity completely because you shared this experience fully in the life of your Son. Help me, Lord, to have insight into what has made the person that I am today. And please help me too, Lord, to begin to overcome my weaknesses in this area of conflict with others. Father, you know the powerful elements at work within me. Please help me to know that transforming power of your Holy Spirit to overcome these difficulties, and please forgive me for all that has been wrong and selfish in what I have said, thought and done. In Jesus Christ's name. Amen.

2

OUR POWERFUL PAST

Conflict is not all the other person's fault. Another figure may be responsible for drawing us out, eliciting all kinds of pained and disagreeable reactions. But the presence within us of pockets of tender vulnerability is a normal part of humanness. Everyone has sensitive areas. The acquisition of these veins of tenderness is an inevitable and legitimate part of our progress towards adulthood and maturity. Yet the existence of such inner 'hot spots' colours and often complicates our reaction to the process and outcome of conflict.

Inner dread

If Frances had not been so low with a cold, maybe she wouldn't have reacted so strongly to Andy, her boyfriend. But when Andy announced he wanted to cool their relationship a little, Frances felt a panic and dread inside which caused her to lash out in unexpected anger. Andy hadn't meant any more than his pressing need to stay in for a few weeks till he had made more headway with his revision. But for Frances the impact of those few words felt like a cold and heartless rejection. It stung her deeply and she recoiled at once.

Andy was surprised at Frances's reaction, particularly as she was normally quite quiet and shy. There was an insecurity in Frances to be sure. Her adoptive parents both feel they have been unable to make up fully for

Frances's childhood abandonment by her mother. As an eighteen-year-old, she still seems to fear rejection. It can make her lash out, sometimes quite irrationally.

Past and present

Frances's past makes a vivid contribution to her present experience. Whatever our past experiences, whether they be noted landmarks or modest signposts, they are always worth considering where conflict is concerned. What we are now has much to do with the way we have steered round or even collided with the obstacles of our lives. So we'll be staying with the subject of the past and the roots of conflict. Later we shall come to look at the practical areas where conflict is most often experienced and what can be done about it. But at the moment it is essential that we work on what we bring with us when we enter these conflict situations. The fact is our unique sensitivities travel with us wherever we go. We cannot ditch them, for we cannot change our past. Our past and present belong together like two sides of the same coin. What we can change is our future. We can change the way we let our past experiences affect us now, so that we are better equipped to handle the impact on us of all kinds of pressure which would otherwise unsettle and upset as time goes on.

Our aim will be to understand and, where appropriate, to modify the *potency* of these feelings and the way we let them affect us when conflicts arise. Such feelings belong to a whole realm of events and reactions often stretching back many years to our earliest days. Many, indeed, are well forgotten by our waking minds. To work hard to clear up any emotional untidiness of this sort is not only beneficial to relationships, in many ways it is essential for healthy living. Given the right circumstances, unattended emotional debris dating from our past can prove quite a stumbling-block. Looking back and sorting out are essential if we are not to experience the pantomime dame's discomfort. Everyone but Widow Twankey sees it coming. She sits down flat and firmly on the pin placed purposely for her displeasure on the bench in the wooded glade. The complaint rings loudly, 'It hurts, it hurts, boo-hoo, it hurts.' We're not surprised at her exclamations. If only she'd looked behind her, she'd have seen how to avoid the discomfort.

Sharp feelings

Our emotional hurts may not always be quite so simple to circumvent. But the sharp and painful reactions we experience in conflict sometimes do have a definite link with experiences of time past. And looking behind us in an emotional sense can be of great preventive value. It's wise to be aware of all the factors which can influence our reactions, and indeed to protect ourselves where possible from needless pain. These tender areas need a good and close scrutiny, if only to avoid the piercing, stinging effects of an unwelcome invasion upon them.

We all cope with past hurts and grievances in different ways. Some have learned to let go and not to dwell on what simply cannot be changed. Others continually hark back. Others still let past wounds so haunt their waking world, they are continually finding emotional parallels in everyday experience, their anger and bitterness becoming recognisable as a definite and unattractive personality characteristic. Others cope with inner pains by building a wall around them. They never let themselves be drawn into any kind of situation where conflict may arise.

Escape measures

Jenny's home had been one of constant arguments and rows. She was an only child and hated her parents' heated exchanges. She would run and hide as her parents' altercations so often got out of hand with plates crashing and books thrown. At first, Jenny took refuge with her dollies and their little friends. Later, as a teenager, under the same stressful circumstances, Jenny would run for her Walkman, drowning the sound of argument with the throbbing beat of rock music.

As an adult, Jenny admits to the same way of coping. She cannot stand conflict: it relives all those half-remembered feelings of fear and dread from years back. It is an escape strategy and she knows it. She runs. She runs as hard as she can from any situation where conflict may arise. This means that she sometimes appears as a person who backs off from intimacy; you never know what Jenny is feeling. She certainly never shows her feelings. Even when her parents eventually divorced, Jenny's closest friends were struck by her apparent calmness and lack of concern. Others might have shown some sadness, regret or even heartbreak.

Evasion tactics

It is both consciously and unconsciously that Jenny uses escape measures to prevent present conflicts from resurrecting old hurts and pains. Escapism isn't just limited to dipping into science fiction or a romantic novel. Evasion of this kind, though most understandable because of the hurt at the root of things, is potentially very dangerous. It not only leaves a catalogue of unresolved hurts, it surfaces in an apprehensive and unrealistic way of coping with present difficulties. It is a constant fear and flight response. Such learned behaviour is heavily ingrained in many of us. We do not always realise what is at the root of our *original* fears, or that we *habitually* cope with conflict in this way at all.

Numerous are the unresolved hurts which lurk in many of us, years after their first appearance in our inner world. As we have already seen, these can be triggered when we are least aware of their presence. Some of us cope by pushing our feelings down, like packing earth firmly into a small flower-pot. But emotions don't like that; they love to have their say. Indeed, they may surprise us. Undealt with ancient hurts may insist on standing up and being noticed.

Because conflict often involves the awareness of being wronged in some way, unresolved past experiences of unfairness, injury or maltreatment can have a powerful effect as we react and respond to more contemporary occurrences.

The wronged self

Peter is the middle child of five. His family were not poor, but in a large household all available resources were fully used in providing for the children. Peter grew up to know the value of money, and was taught by his caring, careful parents to save and be prudent in financial matters, and cautious of whom to trust in business. 'Neither a lender nor a borrower be' was often heard in Peter's house.

Peter didn't really shine at school. He was bright, but a late developer. At sixteen, his father encouraged him to take an apprenticeship in the local handmade furniture shop. Against his father's advice, Peter opted instead for business. He didn't tell his father at the time, but he longed to help his parents financially with his younger brother's and sister's education. He stuck with his ideas, and for a year did all kinds of manual work as a casual labourer till he eventually had amassed enough money to start a grocery business with a friend.

Peter and his partner worked hard together, starting first of all with a stall in Berwick Street market in London's West End. Within twelve months they had bought an old but clean and respectable grocery van to take around the roads of the South London suburbs. Again, this worked well for a while. But when Julian had some money left to him, they decided to pool their resources and go in for something far bigger.

Peter thought it all out very carefully. He decided the wisest course was to pool all he had made over the last two years, enabling Julian to purchase the lease of a high street property. This would enable them to set up a business on a more settled and permanent trading basis. Before long they opened a grocery-cum-delicatessen in a good position as far as passing trade was concerned. Peter's investment was not misplaced. The business did very well with the two lads greatly appreciated locally for their hard work and quality of service. The range of goods they were able to carry was welcomed in the area, as well as lunchtime sandwich facilities which had previously been missing in the neighbourhood.

Success was the fruit of some three years' strenuous work. But it was more than a shock when Julian admitted to Peter that he had been running up huge debts with their bank. Peter knew that Julian gambled, but he hadn't expected him to gamble to that level, and certainly not to use the shop as security. With continual borrowing over two years, the bank had blown the whistle. Everything was gone. Julian was bankrupt. Even if they'd had a formal partnership, which they didn't, it would have made no difference. Peter lost all he'd made, and with it his chance to help his parents and his younger brother and sister, Toby and Laura.

Peter was heartbroken. His father had said all along: 'neither a lender nor a borrower be'. Peter had found out the hard way. But as his mother observed, he was the same Peter, he'd pick himself up somehow. Once again, Peter was resolute. He made up his mind he'd never make the same mistake twice. It wasn't just the money or the hard work, though the waste of that was difficult enough to accept. Peter had been working a debt of love. He'd done all this for his parents, particularly for his father, whose dedication to his children had always impressed Peter and moved him deeply. And now it had all come to nothing.

Peter had wanted to make a response in kind to his parents. As a result, he didn't feel stupid, or incapable in what he'd done. He felt wronged. Deeply, deeply wronged. How could Julian call himself his friend all this time and let him down so badly! It was almost a betrayal. All the more so for, when faced with the facts, all Julian could find to say was, 'Yes, but think how much *I've* lost.'

Doing the dirty

All of us have things we would like to change from the past. If only I *hadn't* said this, that or the other. Peter often felt like that. He nursed his regret for years. He was only nineteen when it all happened. Julian never paid back the money, even though he started up in business again and eventually did all right for himself. Peter never went near him after the bankruptcy case.

A few years later Peter married, settled down and had a family. In the event, he did make some contribution to Toby and Laura's education. It was a great satisfaction to him that they both did well, Toby at teachers' training college, and Laura at polytechnic. It gave him even more pleasure in their latter years to see his parents' joy at their children's happiness, Peter's included.

The angry father

But our interest in Peter's story is represented by a relatively small but important matter which in a negative way affects the happiness of Peter's home life. The question is, what makes Peter such an angry father? Jean, his wife, cannot understand it. His family can't fathom it either. Normally loving and full of fun, Peter can explode with passionate anger at James and Mary, their fourteen-year-old twins. It's usually trivial, like things not being put back in their right place, or borrowing without asking. One day Mary asked her father for money for a pop concert which she had already booked up with a friend without consulting him. The balloon really went up. Mary didn't get hit, but she is adamant that her father *threw* the tray of cups and saucers to the floor and they didn't just fall.

It's been like this over a number of issues ever since the children were small, but it's got worse since they've been teenagers. Yet in casual conversation with the wife of a working colleague, Jean discovers that Peter is just the same at the computer business where he now works as a systems manager. It was a relief to Jean to know that it isn't just the children after all. It appears that Peter often finds himself in conflict. 'He seems so untrusting, so unwilling to let other people get on with things on their own. When someone uses their own initiative, Peter can come on pretty strong. He can seem so threatened, so undermined sometimes. It's almost as though he's afraid they are going to cheat him out of something, or do the dirty on him.'

Alarm bells

The steps of causation in Peter's example are clear enough. But it took a deal of probing when he sought help to ascertain exactly what was the pressure inside Peter, bursting to get out when suitably triggered. Like those alarm systems which are set off when you get too close, Peter could hear the bells' frenzied ringing, but at first he wasn't too clear exactly what posed the threat.

The wrongs we store away are many and varied. There are times in our lives when we are particularly vulnerable and can easily be hurt. School-days mark important growing times in our development. But even in the care of school, emotional traumas are often caused. What may be laughed off by one child may send another into a panic of embarrassment, leaving a legacy of permanent caution in later years.

Put a man down

Ian was not over-bright, but he happened to be popular with the other boys as he was a good footballer and did quite well at sports generally. The eight-year-old Ian had been talking in class all through a painting lesson. His teacher thought he needed a mite of discipline.

Though it was not a particularly good painting, as it happens, Ian had tried especially hard at it; very hard in fact. But to show Ian the detrimental effects of talking when you should be working, Mrs Britten held up Ian's painting in front of the class and systematically ridiculed his efforts; this with Ian standing beside her going redder and redder with every word.

Can't take criticism

It's true that this was not the only experience of ridicule that Ian faced in childhood. And it has to be said that most of us are likely to have some kind of experience when our ego is deflated; and that can often have a beneficial not a negative effect. However, in adult life, Ian finds he cannot take criticism. It stings him. He comes over well as a person, with all the outer confidence you'd expect of a company representative. But he needs constant reassurance. In subtle ways, he seeks praise and affirmation from those he knows it's safe to trust. But when there's criticism of him or his performance, or indeed anything which is linked with him (like his company's products), from customers, his bosses, or even casual acquaintances, Ian finds he cannot cope. On the one hand he feels he wants to run away; on the other he feels his face reddening, and anger welling up. He stops listening to whatever reasonable points might be made. All he can hear is a voice inside him saying, 'Just look at his work. Ian is a lazy, stupid, good-for-nothing.'

Except he doesn't hear those words precisely, he just has a feeling – the emotional impact of an unsteady self-image; unsettled at a formative stage by ridicule and embarrassment.

What's in your catalogue?

There are many issues which affect us. We are all different, and we all react in different ways. When Ian told his wife about the school experience just detailed, Katy said she could hardly believe it mattered that much. And certainly if it had happened to Katy, it probably would have made no impact on her at all. But we are all different in the makeup of our personalities. We all respond in our own unique ways.

So what's in your catalogue of known wrongs? Those memories of yours which cause you pain to think of them. Those injustices, fears, embarrassments, or violations of one kind or another. Is there anything of significance in your past which could in any way contribute to your present reactions in the face of conflict?

Take some moments again to think about this. Note your findings and see what you can discover.

- Can you think of any time in your life when you have been the victim of what you considered to be an injustice, grievance, outrage, or any other kind of wrong?
- Spend some moments thinking over one or more examples of what you have noted, and if you can remember what it felt like at that time.
- Has age mellowed you, or do you still feel something of the vigour of the same emotions?
- Note as many examples now as you can remember where you feel you have been wronged. Irrespective of their magnitude, whether they are big or small, in

each case think about the emotional weight you once gave and still give to them.
- Now build a potency list. With the scale 1 to 10 (10 representing the strongest negative emotions you still feel when you contemplate those occurrences) put a number by each of the events you have listed.
- The next question to ask is about any which have scored 5 or over. Have the 5s and over any connection with what you know of your responses to conflict? Do these issues influence your judgment, trust, concerns or feelings towards any other person, type, or situation?
- Have anxiety, fear, guilt, anger, personal embarrassment or ridicule played a significant part in what you have just been analysing?

The contact points

The connection of past events to present experience of conflict is really crucial. Ask yourself again if there are any contact points between the hurts or wrongs of the past and your present difficulties.

In Peter's case, the whole sad business with Julian had made him jumpy to say the least. Peter is now an extremely suspicious person. He has made himself so by resolving never to make the same mistake twice. He longed to change the past. If only he'd learned the lesson his father had taught him *when* he taught him, *before* it all went wrong. But he was not passive. Instead, he decided to nurse his anger. That would keep the memory bright. He would never forget, he would never forgive. And this time he would stay in control. Nobody would get the better of him.

This is why Peter gets so steamed up with the sales people from the software houses. The cardinal rule in the computer world according to Peter, is: don't trust new programs any further than you can throw them. And that is why Peter's office decided long ago that he was not the person to be first to hear news about the latest software products. Peter had decided in advance that the software houses were likely to rip off his organisation. He therefore gave every enquiring company, irrespective of their experience or worth, very short shrift indeed. Not really the thing for good inter-company relations.

In every other way, Peter is a fine upright and likeable person; he is involved in the Church and is liked and respected locally. But this streak of obsessionality, deriving from his loss all those years ago, not only haunts him, it's made him a remarkably untrusting person even towards his own children. It's the way his past interfaces or connects with the present.

We can see exactly the same connections being drawn in the case of Frances, Jenny and Ian. Frances feels constantly vulnerable to rejection. She is never sure that she is loved. It was learning at an early age that her natural mother had abandoned her which sent the shock waves vibrating through her childhood, adolescence and early adulthood.

In Jenny's situation, the dread of violence and the potential disintegration of her parents' marriage has made her flee from any potential aggression. She even switches off the soap operas on the television when the emotional thermostat gets turned up. Flicking the switch on the TV is one thing, but such reactions are more serious when it comes to real life situations.

With Ian, his inner sensitivity has a negative effect mainly in his working environment. He's very likeable as a person, and this certainly gets him orders, effectively increasing the company's business in the North of England where he lives. But the flip side of that effectiveness is quite clear when things go wrong. When items are faulty, not delivered on time, or more rarely where Ian has by his own fault succeeded in botching an order, then he goes on the defensive. If the customer pushes the point, he fights back. And as a result, he has recently lost two small but important customers, and his sales manager is wanting to know why.

Past hurts and present conflicts

What are the contact points, if any, in your experiences of past hurts and present conflicts? Are there any ways in which you react now to conflict situations which have been affected or constrained by something you have learned from the past? You may not have anything of significance which you can discover, but you should at least give some thought to it; for what we are doing is to clear through, in order to clear away, some of the accumulated emotional jumble of the years. All these elements can exert an influence in some manner or other. What you can do about them is another matter which we shall deal with. The first step is to check what is there in the first place. Use these questions to stimulate your awareness:

- Think back to some recent experiences of conflict. Did any involve the experience of anxiety, fear, guilt, anger or embarrassment within you?
- Now ask what you found most threatening.
- Can you find a link with something in particular that you found intimidating or menacing in the conflict, to anything of significance in your past?
- Do you feel you have fully resolved that situation?
- If not, make a note to work at it, using later exercises in this book.
- Who are the people that you blame for bad things in your life?
- In a conflict situation, have you ever behaved badly towards anyone else; intentionally or unintentionally heaping upon them the blame you attribute to any of the figures you've just thought about and identified?

- Have you ever created a conflict situation yourself with someone you consider responsible for hurting you in some way, perhaps even years before?

Provoking conflict

You would think that most reasonable people would not choose to provoke conflict. We may well not choose to, but if we could be cool, calm and collected and stand back objectively, we might just find that in some conflict situations, to our surprise we may be the unwitting *agent provocateur*. In families, close friendships, and in well-established relationships, this element of provocation can be clearly seen.

Winding the spring

Trevor goes to see his sister about once a month. They usually end up arguing, but they still love each other. Trevor wanted to get married, but never found the right girl. Alison is widowed now and lives on her pension. Trevor winds his sister up. He gets irritated by her fussiness. You see, big sisters sometimes mollycoddle little brothers. Trevor has often wondered whether this made him grow up with silly fussy habits which irritated the girls with whom he would like to have been involved. Alison probably did pamper Trevor, but not as much as he thinks. Their mother was often ill, and Alison, being ten years Trevor's senior, was an enormous help and influence in Trevor's upbringing.

Maybe Alison still treats Trevor as though he wasn't a full-grown adult. Mind you, if you saw the state of his shirts, you might agree that a little mollycoddling was in order. But it makes Trevor simply furious, although he's not a person to show his rage. So like an old-fashioned clock, Trevor simply winds the handle. He doesn't fully realise he does it. But anything he does not like, he criticises. First it's everything being so neat and tidy.

'I don't see why you've got to keep this place as a show house, Alison. I suppose you're frightened of me messing it all up for you, with my dirty boots and all that . . .'

Then it's Alison's insistence on doing the washing-up straight after the meal.

'Can't you just relax for a minute, Alison. You get me all twitched up. Why has everything got to be so squeaky clean as soon as the meal is finished?'

Then it's the one that's bound to annoy.

'You're not going to that church tonight? You practically live in the place. Anyway, Alison, that vicar of yours sounds a real attention seeker. I reckon he's more interested in personal publicity than telling people about God.'

Fully wound, Alison's smoke alarm is triggered. She explodes in a verbal attack on Trevor which momentarily he finds quite a relief. Until, that is, he realises what he has done, and feels cross with himself for walking into an emotional trap of his own unconscious devising.

- Have you ever been in a situation even remotely like this with family, friends, or working colleagues?
- Ask yourself if you remember feeling angry yourself, before the other person showed anger.
- If you were, how did you rub things in?
- Are there any situations where you do this habitually?
- Like Trevor, when the other person's tension breaks and the anger bursts, do you feel any satisfaction or relief within yourself, even for only a few moments?

If you provoke anger in others in this way, part of the explanation is that it is possible to use provocation as a means of releasing your own tension by way of another person. You may not feel able either to explain or express your own anger. The issues may be too delicate to handle or too difficult to put your finger on precisely. So you pass the responsibility, in an almost unconscious way, to the other party. It becomes their responsibility to release the pressure and tension within you. They now become responsible for your anger. It is one of the devious ways in which we all can behave at times. It's not a mature way of behaving. Yet many otherwise mature adults will often behave in this way, mainly because of failure on a long-term basis to deal with anger properly.

The anger response

Anger is not wrong in itself. Indeed the repression of anger can be positively harmful. One psychoanalytic theory of depression is that anger unexpressed and turned inwards is the basic cause of clinically depressive states. But anger has its perfectly acceptable face. This can come as surprise to Christians who have grown up in homes where the expression of anger was frowned upon as being unworthy and sinful. These attitudes, unfortunately, weren't just those of pious Victorians; their presence in many Christian homes today means that youngsters are growing up having to unlearn unbiblical and emotionally unhealthy ways of responding.

Anger in perspective

To get anger in perspective, it helps to see how many positive references there are to anger in the Bible. God himself gets angry. There are references to God's anger throughout the Old Testament. Indeed Psalm 7:11 says that God is angry with the wicked every day. In the epistles of the New Testament, Paul often reminds his readers, as he does in Colossians 3:6, that human sinfulness itself occasions the wrath and anger of God. In the gospels,

Jesus's wholeness as a man is illustrated both by physical and verbal anger on a number of occasions. The expulsion of the money-lenders from the Jerusalem Temple and the overturning of their tables was not expunged by the gospel writers as an unworthy, improper or inappropriate response from Jesus. It was an authentic deed in both senses of the term. In the very strongest language, which can rightly be called anger, Jesus expresses his seven woes against religious leaders who put religiosity before worship of the true and living God (cf. Matt. 23).

So what do we make of the anger response? The unnatural but popular division between righteous and unrighteous anger can get many people in a theological and practical muddle. This is particularly so when you take into account that most people *feel* they are in the right when they are angry, whether they are or not. Yet how can you tell the precise grounds of righteous or unrighteous anger? Our motivations when angry are never wholly pure. How could they be, given the fragmented and fallen nature of our humanness? Of course, there are matters we can get angry about which seem far closer to God's concerns than others. But any minister of even a few years' experience of Christian leadership will be able to tell you of Godly issues which were debated in his Church with a bitterness and rancour totally out of harmony with their subject.

Expressing anger

The object of our anger is, of course, important. We can be angry about the wrong things. We can also fail to be angry about the right things, neglecting issues, say, of justice and truth in our world. But a more important distinction for our purposes is not so much what we are angry about, but how we get angry, how long we remain angry and what our anger response involves. We learn this lesson, as we are surely meant to, from the model of Jesus. His example shows us that it matters *how* our anger is expressed, and that it should not be left to simmer unattended. As James says, anger that is left unresolved 'does not bring about the righteous life that God desires' (Jas. 1:20). But when it is said, 'Do not let the sun go down while you are still angry' (Eph. 4:26) the insight and directive there is immensely practical.

Paul's comment is based on a quotation of Psalm 4:4, 'In your anger do not sin'. In speaking to these early Christians Paul is implying that when they came to follow Jesus, they did not suddenly shed their deepest emotions. If at conversion Christians cast off their ability to be angry, they would shed the whole panoply of their emotional world: their joy, their love, their sense of wonder and awe. Our emotional world is a complete package and it has not been jettisoned. It is, however, meant to be transformed. Paul has just that transformation in mind when he tells the Ephesians to put off the old self, be made new in the attitudes of their minds, and then put on the new self, 'created to be like God in true righteousness and holiness' (Eph. 4:20–4). His steps for transformation are very practical. God does the transforming, we do the co-operating – by letting our lives move in conformity with God's plan for us.

Transformation steps

In using the expression, 'You were taught with regard to your former way of life, to put off your old self . . . ' (Eph. 4:22) Paul is using imagery derived from the picture of changing your clothes. Just as we might buy a new outfit, then take it home and change out of the old and into the new, so Paul likens the complete change needed if we are to live as followers of Christ. We are new people inside, so our outward garments should reflect that. And it is our behaviour which is the visible expression of our new life in Christ. Conscious decisions to live in ways which are consonant with God's will need to be made.

Paul gives some consideration to our attitude to communication within relationships. 'Therefore each of you must put off falsehood and speak truthfully to his neighbour, for we are all members of one body' (Eph. 4:25). Although this refers to a Christian's relationships with other Christians, it is legitimate to extend Paul's principles to all human relationships. What is desirable and wholesome in Christian relationships reflects God's ideal for all.

Paul says, 'Put off your old self, put on the new' (vv. 22,24). The first application of his principle is relational. The putting off involves 'falsehood'. The putting on involves 'speaking truthfully'. All this is set in the context of conflict. For in the very next verse (v.26) Paul says, 'In your anger do not sin. Do not let the sun go down while you are still angry.' What does this tell us in practical terms?

Certainly the references to truth and falsehood can be taken at the simple level of telling the truth and avoiding lies. But the context of the anger response gives Paul's words a deeper dimension still.

- How many people do you know who never show on their faces or reveal in their words what they truly feel?
- To smile when you are angry can be a normal physiological reaction. But how many people do you know who smile broadly at you, and speak in a calm and controlled manner, when all along they are fuming inside and never show it?

That, according to Paul, is 'falsehood'. He's not saying we should explode on the slightest provocation. But in relationships where there are continual small issues which divide, if there isn't some truthful (albeit controlled) expression of the difference, that is how resentments and potential fury can be built up. Those who like Jenny in our case-study find themselves avoiding conflict at all costs, never facing up to issues, never expressing hurt or anger for fear of what it might release in others, need to do some work on this point. Jenny often feels anger, but doesn't show it. And unexpressed anger can cause notable personal problems.

Untangling the past

So what should Jenny do? She should become aware of the pressures of her past which have formed her behaviour in these circumstances. That kind of insight can free her from the constraints of the inner voice which effectively commands her, 'Turn right here. Left here. Stop. Reverse. Quick. Run.' You *can* say no to that inner voice if you know where it comes from and why it says the things it does. That applies to whatever kind of experience you've been through, and whether you're a Frances, a Peter, a Jenny, an Ian or a Trevor.

Paul's point about anger is that anger needs to be expressed and controlled. The context insists that the right object of anger is the one who is its truly justified object. So kicking the cat, biting a towel or pounding a pillow aren't really much use, except for letting off steam. However, if you think your anger is going to get the better of you, then you'd better be realistic and responsible. It's far better to ruin a feather pillow than let yourself overflow in violent behaviour. Coping strategies which are sometimes suggested, like making a mental agreement with yourself or even an actual arrangement with the other party, to stand over an arm's length away and promise not to move from your spot, are sensible if the temperature really soars. The objective, however, is never to let our anger blow up to that extent. 'Do not let the sun go down while you are still angry, and do not give the devil a foothold' (Eph. 4:26–7). Anger needs expression and resolution within a manageable framework of time. Otherwise resentments build up, and anger eventually consumes us with loathing, violent behaviour in words or actions, or destructive decisions towards others. In such ways the devil wheedles his way into human relationships with highly damaging effects.

Dealing with the debris

What should you do about old hurts, the catalogues of personal dramas we have been unearthing in this chapter? The simple directive must be to say 'let go'. Research has shown that the mechanisms in the human brain go through the anger response in less than a second. Of course, we are all too aware of the physiological symptoms which result from anger and which take much more than a second to show their effect and presence: the forehead bunched in a frown, the staring eyes, the constricted pupils, the clenched mouth and fists, the jaw thrust forward, the reddened neck or face and enlarged arteries due to the increase in the blood supply to the skin. But these reactions are a later development when anger has begun to take the system over and commandeer all its ways of expressing displeasure. There is always a moment in time when we can make a decision whether or not to vent our anger. If we bypass the decision we simply move into autopilot and the red alert comes into play.

The brain manages the anger response so quickly because a set mental process is involved. We should not suppress or repress our anger feelings. The reasons we feel hurt or aggrieved (in Paul's terms, the *truth* of the matter) should be faced head on. But the mental process allows us to filter our response to avoid undue rancour. Anger responses can quickly degenerate into self-pity, self-indulgence or self-righteousness; a desire to teach the other person a thing or two – even an exaggerated desire to show that I am right after all, and I told you so!

The balance between self-control and the realistic expression of emotion is difficult to maintain. As we have discovered, to speak falsehood means to suppress feelings as well as truth. Those who go quiet and coy even when offended need to work on this. If we teach ourselves to say what we feel, we'll become known as plain speakers. But be warned. There are many people around who call a spade a spade, but who do so in such a rude, offensive way, that this kind of plain-speaking becomes something to be avoided. Most of us know, or have encountered in some way, an example of someone who speaks his mind, and does so with such gentleness and grace he rarely alienates anyone. If you know someone like that, it's worth observing and studying his or her use of language, manner, and what his body language says to you, even if it is someone you only ever see on television. Similarly, if you ever notice someone having a 'good' positive argument, even if they seem quite passionate, if you are allowed to listen, try and see what keeps it all on the straight and narrow and allows a beneficial and not destructive outcome to be the result.

Letting go of past hurts will be dealt with more fully when we come to Chapter 9. Turn to that chapter now if there are issues you need help with right away. For the moment, ask yourself the following questions.

- Have I discovered there are past hurts within me which still have a dominant role in the way I cope with conflict today?
- With the insight into them which I am developing, am I prepared to let go of my anger, pain and hurt, so that God can heal me of their pain and destructive effects?

Meditate on the words of Paul in Ephesians 4:17–29, asking the Holy Spirit to impress upon your mind where he wants you to make changes to co-operate with him in this work of transformation.

Now use this prayer in any form you wish to bring your thoughts and findings to God.

Thank you, Lord, that you know me through and through. You knew me before I was born. You watch over my coming and going. You've promised you will never let my foot slip. Thank you that the painful experiences I have been through are no surprise to you. You saw them happen, and in your wisdom you allowed them to take place, even though you have deep compassion for my suffering. Help me Lord now to let go of those things where I still nurse anger and resentment, And, loving Father, please bring your gentle healing to my sensitive and painful inner world. Help me to grow and progress from this point on in the way I understand, respond and conduct my relationships with others. For I ask it in the name of Jesus, who himself was not afraid to express anger, but who has taught and shown the world the supreme nature of love. Amen.

3

THE WAY WE SEE THINGS

What I am today is the result of a long process. That process involves a mixture of the interplay between inheritance and learning. It's said that Beethoven had green eyes. *If* he did, the probability is that his genetic inheritance played its part somewhere along the line. Parents with young children are constantly prey to the comments of well-meaning friends and relations convinced that little Freddie's or Jemima's nose, cheek or chin is the spitting image of some great-aunt or other. Whether or not these family resemblances are accurately identified, this kind of inheritance is now firmly established by experience and science. The sharing of genetic coding is very much a family matter.

Family inheritance

The extent to which *personality* characteristics are passed on in this genetic way is less certain. Whatever may be the degree of transference between generations, what is much more clearly established is the high proportion of attitudes and behaviour characteristics unconsciously learned by children and taken right into their adult experience.

They say Anthony looks just like his father. Anthony can never work out why. He has his mother's characteristics, if anyone's, and his mouth and nose are a different shape altogether. But what people notice about Anthony is the way he holds his head down, that he'll hardly ever look you in the eye, and the manner in which he will suddenly turn his whole head away if ever there is disagreement or he is challenged in some way. That's what makes friends who knew his father notice the resemblance. It's the behaviour characteristics which are most striking. Add to those characteristics the meticulous almost fussy ways which Anthony has picked up from his father, and you have a close family likeness – yet to Anthony they are almost completely unacknowledged and unrecognised.

It is common that learned attitudes and behaviour patterns may never be questioned by the grown-up child. Though should such attitudes give rise to negative responses in others, they may then be challenged and with adult maturity undergo some real and positive modification.

What we have inherited will play an important part in our dealings with others, at least as important as the actual experiences we have been through. If my mother was the constantly anxious sort, always worrying unduly about 'what will happen if . . .', then I may turn out to have learned this way of response myself. That learned attitude in its turn may make me uncomfortably edgy and aggressive when situations of uncertainty arise. The aggression may spring from the threat to my inner peace and well-being brought on by the anxiety which I impose unconsciously on the situation.

Anxious moments

My grown-up children are on their way to see me, and in order to do so are having to travel a two-hour journey on the motorway. I am the worrying sort. Without my being in any position to know their movements, they stop off for lunch half-way through their trip. They perhaps take a little longer than anticipated, so when they eventually arrive an hour later than expected, the anxiety has been building up, and I am in a steamy temper.

'I've been so worried. Anything might have happened to you. You can't imagine how anxious I've been. Why didn't you phone?' I am cross and irritable. I bark at anything in sight. And when a few moments later the telephone goes, and the gas man says that he won't after all be coming today to service the boiler, he gets his head bitten off! Under the circumstances, he's unfairly given short shrift.

My window on the world

If I should behave like that, however neurotic and intolerant it may seem, there is nonetheless a consistency and logic to my behaviour. I should have modified my responses and learned to be more in control of my thoughts and tongue. But my reactions were consistent with my learned responses and under-surface fears. Many of our learned perspectives, the way we see things, can have a negative effect; attitudes, preferences and prejudices all play their part in the conflict process. The way we see things is our window on the world. It is bound to affect the way we handle real and potential conflict situations, as much as dislike of fresh air and exercise may contribute to deciding for a family camping holiday or not. It's natural to have likes and dislikes. It's just as natural to have learned patterns of reactions. These are accumulated over many years and may vigorously colour the way we respond to all kinds of situations today.

So we are continuing our analytical path of unearthing as much as is constructive of the part *we* play in the workings of conflict. We have already looked at some aspects of what makes each one of us the distinctive, uniquely individual people that we are. We've learned of those features of our life stories which potentially contribute negatively to conflict situations. We've also remembered again the sometimes potent hurts of time gone by, realising that the passing years do not always lay to rest the stretched emotional reactions which those experiences once forced upon us. In all this, we've discovered a definite link between what has made us what we are and the unsettling elements which we now bring as responses or even confrontations when conflict arises.

Personal philosophy

But it is not just the *events* of the past which exert their influence on our relationships with others. Everyone has some kind of world view. We all look at things in different ways. A personal philosophy is something which all people have no matter what their background, class, or educational attainment. The 'grand' world view is the presence or absence of a religion which we openly or privately espouse. That belief system will be accompanied by values of behaviour and culture, which we are likely to accept and practise to a greater or lesser degree. For some, politics and political thought and action can be an important element within their 'grand' world view, and may be part of their religious or humanist convictions. But one step down from this grander world view at a more personal level, we all have a simpler way of seeing things which still vigorously affects the shape and colour of our personalities and what contributions and responses we bring to our relationships with others. These ways of seeing, though possessing many positive characteristics, when robustly held can provide a fertile seedbed for the growth and development of conflict reactions and responses.

Strong-minded

Muriel had applied to a firm of insurance brokers for a job as an administrator-cum-personal assistant to one of the three senior partners. Now in her early fifties she may find her age an advantage for the stability, maturity and experience she could bring to the position. There were ten applicants for the job, all with suitable qualifications, some much younger than Muriel. After some careful sifting on the basis of ability and experience, Muriel was eventually short-listed with two other applicants. Though she'd never worked in insurance, her potential employers thought her smiling manner and evident efficiency would equip her well for the task, particularly as she appeared a quick learner, and did well in the practical assignment they gave her during the period of the interview itself. Muriel had the impression she was a strong contender for the position. So when the personnel officer told her she'd be hearing from them in the next two days, Muriel went away optimistic.

The firm took up references on all the candidates interviewed. Those handling the interviews did not have the chance to discuss their observations of the candidates till later that day. All three candidates were acceptable on the face of it. Muriel, probably because of her years and the fact they were looking for a more mature person, was by a hair's breadth the front-runner, ahead of two younger girls both with experience of the insurance business. Muriel was favoured by all three partners, but the comments of her present employer turned out to be of particular importance. The personnel officer read out the relevant paragraph:

> Muriel is a hard worker and does well when working on her own. Her initiative, efficiency and intelligence are beyond question. She has achieved a great deal, and made a valuable contribution to our company's efficiency over these last seven years. In many ways we shall be very sad to see Muriel go. But you asked me to comment on potential weaknesses, and this is one area which you may consider to be worthy of some serious attention.

Muriel is a single-minded person. This is one of the reasons she works well with tasks she has to achieve on her own. But when working with others she may appear a little inflexible. Someone here once commented that she gives the impression she always seems to know best. For this reason I have to say we have not been too happy with her work on joint projects. She has definite ideas on how she thinks things should be organised, and sometimes she is right. But she does not take kindly to criticism. She also seems to think some of the younger girls in the office have no right to thoughts of their own. I don't think it has anything to do with her age, for I think it is just part of her personality. Though this following comment may not affect her work performance as such, Muriel is a person with strong views generally, particularly about religion. She is as honest and upright as they come, but has landed like a ton of bricks on younger members of staff whose behaviour she doesn't approve of. If I tell you she is known by some here as 'Aunty' Muriel, you may get the picture. I'm afraid on more than one occasion, she's had one or two of the girls in tears. But that said, Muriel is a good person and a hard worker. If you want her to work closely in a team, you may wish to give some thought to the matters I have mentioned.

There are some aspects of our personalities which may not come over in the brief span of an interview, but which those close to us know only too well. Family, friends or working colleagues see us more clearly than we realise. We may keep certain parts of ourselves well hidden from view, but our behaviour can speak volumes about attitudes, preferences and prejudices, some of which can be important when it comes to dealing with disputes and differences of opinion or possible action. Unfortunately, what may appear obvious to all but ourselves, even our best friends don't tell us.

THE WAY WE SEE THINGS

Maybe it is feasible for you to find someone who knows you well enough to comment (friend, family or colleague) and to give you some personal insights. You'll have to be brave to do it, but what you may learn from this will be well worth the effort!

We are going to analyse responses to people and ideas. As an illustration of what we are trying to unearth, let's go back to Muriel's situation again, and think of her in relation to this exercise.

Muriel (who didn't get the job) holds strong views. As her employer said, she is a person of very significant worth. But this is the time to think of the weaker side. Muriel's attitude to others in a working environment gives little credit to anyone else for practical intelligence or reliability. This shows in the way she bustles around at coffee time, often scowling (though she doesn't realise it), peering over the work of others, like a strict teacher in a class of rowdy twelve-year-olds. Out of the office, Muriel's preferences are for classical music, a quiet existence, with knitting, visiting the elderly and church on Sundays pretty well top of the list.

Muriel opposed planning permission for the new community centre opposite her flat. But despite her strenuous objections, the building went ahead. They have an open youth club with a drop-in disco once a week on a Friday night. Muriel really can't abide the sound of pop music, and she has managed to get the club to agree that the music must finish at 10 p.m. The community-centre members are conscious of the need for good relationships with their neighbours, and have bent over backwards to accommodate Muriel. Yet the two local authority community workers know the sharper side of Muriel's tongue. If the music should go on past 10 o'clock for even a minute or two, Muriel is out and about. If only she could see the good work they are doing there among young people. But Muriel writes off these youngsters with their strange clothes and weird hairstyles as if they were a lower kind of creature altogether. As someone who came from a happy, steady home, she might be able to offer help in some small way to some of these disadvantaged youngsters, a few of whom hardly know what it is to be loved at all. As it is, she has resisted all attempts of the club to involve local residents in these community-related activities, even when they offered to clean her car and windows free!

Gaining insight

When Muriel didn't get the job she'd hoped for she talked it over with her present boss. She had been completely open about testing the waters as far as a change of job was concerned. She asked her head of department if he could think of anything which might have acted against her. Sensibly, but with some sensitivity, her boss made the same points to Muriel as he had made in his reference, asking her at the same time if these conflicts had ever arisen out of the office with family friends or neighbours. Before long Muriel spoke of these strains with neighbours and other personal tussles in her life. Her employer commented frankly, but with great gentleness, on his observations of Muriel's way of handling others, particularly when conflict arose. Some years later, Muriel admits that this conversation was the making of her. These were aspects of herself which she had only half perceived. She had neither been in control of them, nor was fully aware of their erosive influence on her relationships with others. It took a fuller self-knowledge to do something effective about them.

- Make a list of what you believe to be your own specific, characteristic and strongly held views in terms of attitudes, preferences, and prejudices. For each of these you should mention responses to people and ideas.
- Some of your views and personal characteristics will be positive. What are they?

THE WAY WE SEE THINGS

- Some of your views and characteristics will turn out to be negative. What are they?
- Before moving on to the next step, write yourself a character reference for a job. Be frank, truthful and uncompromising. What would you say about yourself, supposing that you write as an objective outsider who knows you well?
- Now ask a friend to do the same analysis of your attitudes, preferences and prejudices. Ask them to be as specific as possible, and not hold back on any areas, even if they seem embarrassing. Say something like, 'I promise not to get cross if you hit on the truth!' and encourage honesty, as well as sensitivity.
- Compare your findings together, asking your friend to explain how they have noticed these aspects of your personality in practice, and what they consider the most destructive, damaging elements in what they have described (if any) and why. Then show the reference and see if they recognise the real you in it.

The distortions of prejudice

Attitudes represent the way we see things; preferences the way we like things to be; prejudices the way we potentially distort what we see. Prejudice is by definition a strongly held view, often lacking flexibility. Prejudice may therefore contribute to conflict in many different ways. The lives of countless millions of people have been made a misery through the conflicts arising from prejudice. And in recent history the existence of prejudice has led to both large-scale violence and genocide, as the Holocaust so dreadfully illustrates. Yet the distortions of prejudice can have subtle effects on people's behaviour. There are times when prejudice only contributes to conflict in the narrow band of outlook and experience where that prejudice exists.

Check-out girl

Phyllis is in active retirement, a fit, energetic and well liked sixty-seven-year-old. She's well regarded, except at times in her local supermarket where Phyllis occasionally undergoes something of a personality change. Phyllis is very particular about cleanliness, which is why she always shops at the new branch of Safeways. Ever since she gave up full-time employment where everyone touched their cap to her, she's found the loss of identity difficult to cope with. She finds it warming that the check-out girls give her a smile and a 'Good morning, Mrs Evans' when she passes through. Her insistence on cleanliness made her work as a director of a local laundry extra successful, and the company did well with her important contribution. But a check-out line is not the place for the kinds of confrontation senior management might need to have on the shop floor!

When Safeways was particularly busy one Friday lunchtime, Phyllis popped in for a packet of chops for her husband and herself. The check-out clerks normally pack the already neatly wrapped fresh meat for you in a plastic bag. As it happened, the chops were beginning to drip, and there was a long line of people waiting behind Phyllis. Phyllis had never seen the check-out girl before. She looked Asian, the only Asian on the check-out that day, and she was taking her time as she was still learning her way around.

Phyllis didn't like the look of her. And when she didn't wrap the item in a bag, Phyllis was furious. It was just the excuse she needed to get stroppy. Her racially prejudiced views didn't help the matter, but it was what she was thinking rather than what she said which added flame to the fire of her anger. While everyone waited irritatedly behind her, Phyllis insisted on calling for the supervisor. She wanted an explanation. She wasn't going to move till she got one. Why had the item been left unwrapped? She made quite a fuss. She was listened to very politely.

She certainly got her apology from the supervisor. The mystified check-out girl was understandably hurt.

Other people's prejudices are not difficult to discern, even though they may not come right out with it. The other customers were almost as hot under the collar as Phyllis, but for very different reasons! Phyllis enjoyed telling all that had happened for some days. But in spite of her enthusiasm, she never tumbled to the silent response which greeted her each time she told the story.

Such incidents happen with greater or lesser degrees of seriousness at regular intervals in all our lives. It is easy to be critical of prejudice in the lives of others, particularly when it is as small minded as that of Phyllis. But there may have been incidents where we have been involved. We may be ashamed of what we've said or done. Prejudice may lead us into aggressive attitudes towards some person or group.

Spoiling for a fight

The *desire* for aggression is a significant factor in conflict. Some people simply love a fight. They want to be vindicated. They want to be proved right. They can't bear to lose. They'll be like a dog with a rag, tugging away at it, with growls and grunts till you loosen your hold and let them have their rightful trophy.

- Can you think of examples of how something like this has happened to you?
- What part was played by your attitudes, preferences and prejudices?
- What kind of person are you in conflict situations? Do you rise to the bait? Are you the sort who can't bear to lose an argument, or to be proved wrong; or do you mentally creep away from the conflict and experience all its discomfort within yourself.

- Why do you think you are like this? Are there elements in your upbringing, or the character of your parents or others close to you from whom you have learned, which help to explain or cast light on who you are and how you behave and respond, given certain circumstances?

Many of us laugh at prejudice when it is presented to us in someone else. Even Phyllis's racial prejudice might have had a touch of the humorous about it, if it weren't so offensive and pathetic. Why is it that prejudice is sometimes a successful vehicle for comedy? Dame Edna Everage, the outrageous creation of Australian Barry Humphries, is the epitome of prejudice. She is as bigoted as they come, but the laughter is deafening. Perhaps the reason for the comic success of such characters is that they help us to recognise the prejudice which exists in all of us at so many different levels about so many different things. Out in the real world, if these things weren't so serious, they would indeed be laughable.

First-century perspectives

The New Testament describes the presence and effects of prejudice, and in strong terms describes the way in which it can contribute to conflict. Because of the existence of such prejudice among the early believers, it should not surprise us that prejudice will, and does, exist in churches today. Christians are no more immune to the subtle influences of prejudiced attitudes than they are exempt from inclinations towards selfishness, greed or envy. Prejudice is another human weakness, and like our emotions does not disappear at conversion.

Luke, the writer of the gospel and the book of Acts, is at pains to expose prejudice, especially religious prejudice, and to show the difference the transforming work of

Christ makes on the mind where issues of prejudice are at stake.

The Gentile conflict

The book of Acts is about the spread of Christianity after the resurrection and ascension of Jesus, through the giving of the Holy Spirit, empowering Jesus's followers in making his good news known. A turning-point in the book comes in Acts, chapter 10, where the mission of making Jesus known turns a corner, and the non-Jewish world, the Gentiles, are included in God's salvation plan. In this chapter, there are two visions. In the one, Cornelius, a Roman centurion, is prompted by God to seek out the Apostle Peter. And in the other Peter is taught by God that he is no longer to abide by the old Jewish distinctions of clean and unclean. Even Gentiles are included in God's dealings with mankind. Cornelius and his whole household are Gentiles. They respond personally to Peter's message about Jesus, the Holy Spirit comes on them and they are baptised. The family of Cornelius are therefore the first non-Jews to become known as followers of Christ, and this was a highly significant moment in the life of the early Church. It occasioned a great deal of comment and controversy at the time. For Peter to get himself involved with Gentiles was not only a controversial act, it required a full and sufficient explanation to his outraged critics.

Peter's explanation of his actions is against the background of conflict and prejudice. 'The apostles and the brothers throughout Judea heard that the Gentiles had also received the word of God. So when Peter went up to Jerusalem, the circumcised believers criticised him and said, "You went into the house of uncircumcised men and ate with them" ' (Acts 11:1–3).

There is a real sense of surprise embedded in the way that Luke deals with this issue of conflict, taking two whole chapters to expound it. The surprise would have been obvious to his original readers. For the Gentiles to receive the word of God, at this point in history, was a truly extraordinary thing to happen in the eyes of those who had been used to years of prejudice against the Gentiles. Up to this point, all the earliest followers of Jesus were Jews. The Pharisees had taught that Gentiles were anathema and an abomination to God. It took some getting used to the idea that Gentiles were fellow-heirs in God's kingdom, brothers and sisters in the same family, for there was a great deal of prejudice against the Gentiles.

The Gentile prejudice

Gentile simply means non-Jewish. In the Old Testament, Gentiles are regarded very positively. God has a definite plan for the Gentiles. Isaiah declares that God's servant, whom Christians recognise as Jesus Christ, will be 'a light for the Gentiles' and that God himself 'will "beckon" them, calling them forth to be part of his purposes of salvation to the ends of the earth' (Isa. 42:6;49:6,22). But human attitudes can harden, and beyond the Old Testament we see those human prejudices taking shape. By the time of the New Testament, those hardened attitudes are positively aggressive; so much indeed that 'Gentile' in itself actually becomes a term of abuse. Today we find the equivalent in talking offensively and insultingly about coloureds, niggers, fuzzy-wuzzies, chinks, yids and so forth.

The Gentile threat

For Peter this prejudice erupts into a situation of conflict. 'When Peter went up to Jerusalem, the circumcised believers criticised him and said, "You went into the house of uncircumcised men and ate with them" ' (Acts 11:2–3). 'Uncircumcised men' is another way of referring to the non-Jewishness of the Gentiles. But the accusation of eating with the Gentiles has been heard before, for Luke records the Pharisees' earlier complaint about Jesus, '"This man welcomes sinners and eats with them"' (Luke 15:2). For Peter the change in understanding was critical. 'I now realise ... that God does not show favouritism but accepts men from every nation who fear him and do what is right' (Acts 10:34–5). Prejudice is a strange and irrational matter. The fact that both Jesus and Peter upset their critics by eating with Gentiles is comprehensible in terms of the violation of Jewish law. But law apart, why were people so threatened when Jesus and Peter associated with non-Jews?

Twisting truth

As we have already discovered, many of the problems we face are related to the way we see things, our world view. Those who have a strongly held 'grand' world view, with a convinced belief in God and a set of related moral values, are vulnerable at this point. Strong world views, such as strong religious beliefs, imply strong sets of associated values. When truth gets distorted so do the values that go with it.

The Pharisees who appear in the gospels in Jesus's time seem to have some distorted ideas about God. In spite of all the evidence from Abraham onwards, they apparently believed that God writes off anyone who does not belong to the actual nation of Israel. It's like the attitude that you have to be good and religious, think the right thoughts, wear the right clothes, believe the right things, come from the right background, if you are in any way to be acceptable to God.

The Jewish Christians had just as distorted an idea of God and by consequence had run into problems in their relationships with these brand-new non-Jewish converts. These distortions are the very essence of prejudice, and it is hardly surprising that conflict with Peter had arisen.

Righting the record

Peter's manner of dealing with conflict is itself instructive. His response is not one of evasion or confrontation, but of explanation. He faces the issue and chooses to explain the vision he had received which led to his actions in making himself known to these despised Gentiles. In a Christian response to conflict, the embrace of right doctrine should eventually lead to right action. For the truth of God in the power of the Spirit can shed light and liberate where the simple recognition of fault or personal deficiency lacks power for transformation.

'Peter began and explained everything to them precisely as it happened' (Acts 11:4). He unfolds the vision. That which once was unacceptable as far as the old Jewish food laws were concerned, can now be accepted. The voice from heaven declares, 'Do not call anything impure that God has made clean' (Acts 11:9). It is stated three times, driving the message home. When God's word on some matter comes to us in repeated form in different ways, it is worth reflecting whether we are really attending to the influence it is intended to have upon our beliefs and behaviour. Peter clearly took to heart what must have been a challenging and potentially testing message. He must have known the looks of bewilderment, horror and disbelief that he would receive from some, and even the militant hostility that might await him when his visit to the Gentile, Cornelius, was discovered.

The prejudice of several centuries is about to take a tumble. If as the vision had suggested, non-kosher *food* can no longer pollute, neither will contact with non-Jewish *people* pollute. That is the main thrust of the vision. But if you were Jewish, and had grown up in a strict kosher home it might be difficult to accept, even if you now had a broader view through your conversion to Christ. Imagine yourself in that position. You are told that all these ritual practices have now come to an end, for the coming of Jesus makes all ceremonial redundant. Practices which have characterised the details of your daily living from the cradle upwards are dealt a swift and final blow.

Too old to change?

You might start complaining that all these changes are happening too rapidly for comfort. Human beings do not like change, especially as they get older. Certainly to change the patterns of a lifetime is bad enough, but what about changing your beliefs? Peter says that the Holy Spirit has come upon the Gentiles. From Luke's description of the response, some thought of that as an outrage. Aren't the Gentiles condemned by God's law? Peter's initial step in correcting this prejudice is to correct the doctrine, the way his fellow converts thought about God and his ways. The fact that the Holy Spirit has come upon the Gentiles is a sign from God that the Old Testament plan for the Gentiles is coming to fulfilment after all. After a lifetime of distorted thinking, it is not easy to change your prejudices. Peter's approach is highly instructive.

When Peter saw the evidence that the Holy Spirit had come upon the Gentiles, the words of Jesus came to his mind. '"Then I remembered what the Lord had said: 'John baptised with water, but you will be baptised with the Holy Spirit.' So if God gave them the same gift as he gave us, who believed in the Lord Jesus Christ, who was I to think that I could oppose God?"' (Acts 11:16–17).

Unseating prejudice

The prejudiced often write off whole groups of people as being unacceptable. The excuse is often a religious one: they are unacceptable to God. That's the position of many white South Africans. Some South African Dutch reformed theologians claim Scriptural support for the outrageous assertion that blacks are an inferior race of people. It's been their justification for apartheid. The arguments are specious, yet all the more odious, because the gospel of Jesus Christ actually deals with prejudice in a very deep way.

God's truth is meant to have a powerful effect in changing even the most deep seated of our attitudes, even attitudes like those of the early Jewish Christians towards the Gentiles which had centuries of cultural back-up to support them. When Peter makes the point that the non-Jews have received exactly the *same* gift of the Holy Spirit as the Jewish Christians, the logic is inescapable. This is the true gospel, the love and acceptance of God is for all people, irrespective of their background or history. It is for the good, the bad and the ugly; the religious, the pagans, and the don't-cares.

Slow learners

Why does Luke spend two whole chapters in the Acts of the Apostles bringing considerable weight to this matter to make his point? In the early Church the evidence suggests that Christians were slow to come into line with God's actual purposes in the gospel. Some years after these events, at Galatia, Colossae and Corinth, there are clear indications that those in the Church prejudiced against Gentiles tried to impose circumcision and other aspects of the Jewish law upon new converts. They weren't too quick to give up their prejudices, for part of the reason for the existence of prejudice is that our intolerance is directed against those who form some kind of threat to us.

The emotions of prejudice therefore run deep. The fears they embody need dealing with just as much as the wrong thinking they exhibit. It is one matter being told you should deal in a different way with the person you dislike or despise, yet another to know what to do with strong emotions you experience in relation to these people.

Fighting fear

So what can we do about fears in relation to prejudice? The New Testament declares that perfect love, God's perfect love, drives out fear from within (1 John 4:18). The problem was then, as it is today: many only pay lip service to what the love of God actually means. We impose conditions on others where the love of God would impose no conditions at all. We do it in every realm of life, but it can be more clearly seen when it happens in community groups of one kind or another. Churches are places where these prejudices are particularly noticeable.

> Our congregations demand from every new member not only a conversion but also a change in culture. He has to abandon some of his contemporary behaviour and to accept the older patterns prevalent among the majority of the congregation. The new Christian has to learn the old hymns and to appreciate them. He has to learn the language of the pulpit. He has to share in some conservative political opinions. He has to dress a bit old-fashioned . . . In brief, he has to step back two generations and undergo what one may call a painful cultural circumcision (*God's Lively People*, Fontana, 1971).

These biting and critical words come from those writing from within the Church, and the fact they were written some twenty years ago has not, lamentably, altered their truth and pertinence. We can smile, yet at the same time feel the sting of such a recognition of discrimination, intolerance and bigotry. Dame Edna Everage may make us laugh at prejudice, but are we smiling or laughing at ourselves? Many of us fail to realise just how prejudiced we can be, for our prejudices can take on very subtle forms.

The Church of today has problems with prejudice in both subtle and blatant ways. In the time of Acts, real and deep-seated prejudice was dealt with by a clear commitment to the terms and truth of the good news of God as God himself declares it to be. After Peter explains the equal spiritual standing of the non-Jewish Christians, this is the response: 'When they heard this, they had no further objections and praised God saying, "So then, God has granted even the Gentiles repentance unto life"' (Acts 11:18). Whatever the inner pressures within us to hold on to a prejudicial attitude, when a Christian maintains a prejudice and fails to aim for its resolution, the problem may well be a conflict with God's truth, of actually resisting God's will.

What me, prejudiced?

The question 'How prejudiced am I?' is a hard one. It searches my attitudes not just to blacks, gays, AIDS victims or the lepers of our society, like the down-and-outs, drug addicts and others. It also challenges my attitude to the more superficially respectable, whom we simply do not want to get on with, and strive earnestly to keep at arm's length. Some people ignore and 'send to Coventry' individuals they disapprove of. Others will only ever maintain the minimum levels of civility in their dealings with certain individuals. Then there are those who always have a harsh word for another. All these attitudes are based on deep-seated prejudice and cause conflict.

The silent feud

Janet, Audrey, Elizabeth and Max were a happy and united family. They grew up together, though Elizabeth was considerably younger than the other three. Their father died some years ago, leaving their mother a widow, though well provided for. When, some twenty years later, she became ill and eventually died, there was some unfortunate squabbling over the will.

THE WAY WE SEE THINGS

Elizabeth had lived with her mother all these years. She was the only one of the children never to have married. It came as a blow to her that her eldest sister, Audrey, and brother, Max, had sold off many of their mother's belongings without so much as a by-your-leave. This left its mark, with squabblings about the will and its terms taking their toll in many bitter arguments.

For years to come, Elizabeth was almost ostracised by her two older sisters. It took the death of Max to bring them together again on speaking terms. Even then the old resentments weren't far from the surface.

Janet's comment to Audrey gave some insight into the feud. 'What Elizabeth doesn't grasp is that none of us can stand the fuss she makes. She can be so vindictive in what she says. I'd rather run the mile than face Elizabeth in one of her tempers. She really frightens me.'

Resolving prejudice

To resolve such attitudes, in the end it has to be a question of transformation. Every one of us has prejudices of some kind in varying degrees. Some result from experiences or preferences, and are reactions to our fears or those we feel are some kind of threat to us. To be free of such fears we need to let God's love drive that fear out.

- Is there any person or persons against whom you feel a real or active prejudice?
- Can you say what it is about them that threatens you?
- What are the emotions that you feel as you think about them?
- There may be some family conflict, some ongoing difficulty with a relation or one-time friend. Are you prepared in the light of God's desire for your wholeness to let go of whatever negative emotions you have towards them?

There can be no doubt that God wants to help you deal with these conflict-producing attitudes. The wilfulness of human nature can be deceitful, and we can hang on to old ways like cherished thoughts or possessions. That's not God's best for you. Ask the Holy Spirit to give you the strength and resolve to follow God's will in whatever he has been revealing to you. You may like to think quietly for a few moments, then read these words from the first letter of John.

> There is no fear in love. But perfect love drives out fear, because fear has to do with punishment. The one who fears is not made perfect in love. We love because he first loved us. If anyone says, 'I love God,' yet hates his brother, he is a liar. For anyone who does not love his brother, whom he has seen, cannot love God, whom he has not seen. And he has given us this command: Whoever loves God must also love his brother (1 John 4:18–21).

After you have had time to think over John's words in relation to yourself, use this prayer to help you deal with any of the negative attitudes and prejudices you have discovered within yourself in this chapter.

Father in heaven, I thank you for your great love which banishes fear from my life. Your word speaks powerfully to me not only of your love but of your will. I now bring before you all the attitudes I now realise to be wrong. Please forgive me these things and the people I have wronged. Lord, you understand why I have been as I have. Help me to know a new start and a new strength as I seek to repair the wrong I've done. And I do so in the desire to serve you and in the power of the Holy Spirit. In Jesus's name. Amen.

Part Two

Interpersonal Conflict

4
FAMILY RELATIONSHIPS

Won't be a minute ...

'Sarah, what are you doing in that bathroom?'
 'I'm washing, Mum. I'll be out in a minute.'
 'Sarah, I'm going to be late for my meeting. Please hurry up.'
 'All right, Mum. All right. I won't be long.'
 'Sarah, what on earth are you doing in there? It's not your bathroom, you know. Why don't you think about others for a change?'
 'I told you, Mum, I'll be out in a minute.'
 'Look, Sarah, I'm late.'
 'M-u-m. Just hold on a bit, won't you? I said I won't be a minute.'
 'Sarah, I need to get washed.'
 'Sarah?'
 'Mum, I'm doing my best.'
 'Sarah, if you don't hurry up I'll have to get your father to get you out of there.'
 'Sarah. Will you answer me? Sarah. Sarah.'
 A moment's silence. Then a crash. Wood hits plaster. The bathroom door flies open. Sarah flounces out. Then the truth.
 'Mother, why is it you're always hassling me?'

Frustration

Families can be very frustrating. In the above scenario the frustration is not so much about who uses the bathroom first; that's just the surface issue. The real gut feelings go far deeper. 'Mother, why are you always hassling me?' That's the frustration which got to Sarah. Frustration lies at the heart of many of the arguments, squabbles and difficulties which families experience. So what can snappy families do to resolve the frustrations in their interpersonal relationships which may give rise to verbal fights, bitter conflicts and destructive hostilities?

Parental modelling

In the first section on interpersonal conflict we are going to concentrate on the mutual relationship of parents and children. Childhood provides a vital formative stage for development. As we discovered in Part One, many of the initiators of conflict in later life are learned and impressed upon us at this vital period. One reason for the New Testament's concern for the quality of family life is that our development into mature humanness relies on a complex and subtle learning-process. This process involves the combination of love and discipline in a secure and balanced family environment where both parents are present to contribute to a child's development into maturity.

In Britain some 14 per cent of families with dependent children are headed by a lone parent, and figures for one-parent families are on the increase in Britain and the USA. Families in these situations need particular understanding and support, for it is not easy for wider family and friends to act as effective substitutes for the role of the missing parent. Much of the controversy which has raged over the issue of AID (Artificial Insemination by Donor) revolves around this issue. The question of the absolute right of a woman to bear a child needs offsetting by the right of a child to a balanced upbringing. That balance is achieved best with the presence of *both* role models, not only for psychosexual stability, but also for the learning process of which harmonious and healthy conflict management is a part.

Parents and children

It is not difficult to see the reasons for the Bible's crucial emphasis on right parental modelling. These are some of the clearest concerns of God for our lives, running uncontradicted through Old and New Testament alike. In one central passage the Apostle Paul brings together the essence of this teaching from both Testaments, and with some clearly articulated principles lays down teaching which has many straightforward and practical applications for the frustrations and conflicts which many families experience today.

> Children, obey your parents in the Lord, for this is right. 'Honour your father and mother' – which is the first commandment with a promise – 'that it may go well with you and that you may enjoy long life on the earth.' Fathers, do not exasperate your children; instead, bring them up in the training and instruction of the Lord (Eph. 6:1–4).

Family life is hard work. It may be full of happiness for those who are fortunate to have the right conditions at play in their lives, but there is no doubt how stretching it can be to live in close proximity to your relations.

Mother and daughter

A family doctor often finds himself a father confessor as much as a physician. On Tuesdays, Dr Jacks takes both a morning and an afternoon surgery. There'll be a whole range of needs, many uncomplicated, others requiring the most careful attention.

This particular Tuesday Georgina Taylor came in looking tired and drawn. At fifty-three she has had some minor medical problems, but is usually fit and healthy. 'Will you check my blood pressure please, doctor? I've been feeling headachy and dizzy for a few days now.'

The blood pressure was checked and yes, it was a little higher than last time. Not too much to worry about though.

'Is anything bothering you, Georgina?'

After a moment's pause, Georgina feels her emotions getting the better of her. 'It's Mandy. She's so rude and ungrateful for everything we do. She's going out with this man who is thirteen years older than her. He's nice enough, but she won't be fifteen till next month. And she just shouts and screams and upsets everyone. All she seems able to say is, "Don't tell me what to do, I can look after myself." Well, all I can say is that the strain is driving Jim and me to distraction . . .'

Points of view

It just so happened that Mandy turned up at the afternoon surgery. Dr Jacks decided his first task was to listen to Mandy independently and find out the reason for her visit.

Mandy had come because she was worried about her parents and she didn't know who else to turn to. But what a difference a change of view makes.

'You see Mum and Dad don't stop nagging me. They issue continual threats. "If you don't do as we say, we'll stop your swimming coaching. If you don't stop seeing Mark now we won't support you when it comes to further education." And it's not just my boyfriend. My dad is always goading me. He doesn't like the way I dress.

He doesn't like my friends. He doesn't like the places I go at weekends. He doesn't like the music I play in my room. I can't do anything to please him. The mad thing is I love him. I love them both. But you wouldn't think so from the arguments we have. I sometimes want to throw things at them. I did this morning. It was just a plate. I threw it on the floor. It bounced. But it could have been a whole smashed-up dinner service for the row it caused.'

Snappy families

Arguments, rows, temper tantrums, thrown objects. This is the lot of many families. It is hardly surprising when the pressures of growing up are considered. But it is easier to cope with these pressures if we go back to first principles. It is important in any situation to understand the purpose of any activity in which you are involved; then you can make decisions more clearly in line with that purpose, and develop strategies consonant with its goals. So to understand the overall purpose of family life, we must gain an understanding of its principles, and this in turn will help us to cope with its inevitable pressures and conflicts.

Family goals

The Bible refers in many places to the importance of the home environment. Rather than the carpets, curtains and video, this refers to the quality of relationships which should exist between parents and children. That quality is not inherent in us, like being born with beautiful blue eyes or a lovely skin, so that some people naturally have good relationships and others equally naturally do not. The quality of relationships the Bible speaks of in terms of the home environment is learned and therefore needs to be practised. Like the difference between phrase-book French and fluent speech, it is largely a matter of hard work, learning and regular application. The relationship between parents and children can never be taken for granted. Harmonious family life requires regular maintenance, and adjustments of understanding as one phase of development gives way to another. Thus the simple but overall goal is that children should grow up properly equipped for adult life.

The learning relationship

This essential learning process is relational, for adult life and behaviour are lived out in a wide range of relationships. Thus the learning context of any child must initially be the loving home where relationships can be tried out in all kinds of ways, mistakes made, lessons noted and adjustments effected. This process is Paul's main thought behind each of his directives. He speaks to children with a principle, a command and a promise.

The principle

When Paul says in Ephesians, 'Children, obey your parents for this is right', he is referring, as he often does, to a creation principle. That principle is implied in the expression 'for this is right', meaning that obedience is part of the maker's instructions. It is 'right' in the sense of being a natural part of the way we have been made.

On all kinds of goods these days you see a manufacturer's endorsement, 'Success only guaranteed if maker's instructions adhered to.' According to Apostle Paul that kind of guarantee applies equally to growing up. Obedience is part of the maker's instructions, and there is no guaranteed success without it; for obedience is a God-created way of ensuring that we learn the right

FAMILY RELATIONSHIPS

habits of living in our early years. To use Paul's word, it is 'right' in the sense of being natural for our human development.

Victorian values?

For some, of course, the whole idea of obedience is old-fashioned, Victorian and irrelevant. Certainly the demand for obedience can be open to abuse. But just because something can be used wrongly doesn't mean that it is wrong in itself. Parents can abuse their right to expect obedience. Parents can be wrong in the obedience they ask for. Mandy's parents had been understandably concerned at her friendship with Mark, but their demands on her had been bordering on the unreasonable. Their attitude had certainly contributed to, not lessened, the family conflict. But there are different kinds and qualities of obedience. The obedience envisaged by Paul is not the obedience of a slave. It is the obedience of willing co-operation.

Family demands

Janice and Ken have three children. Ken's job in the library often leaves him tired and touchy at the end of a day. The family strategy is that Daddy mustn't be disturbed when he comes in at six. The news is on TV, the cup of tea made. No one speaks till the news is over and Ken's cobwebs have been well and truly blown away.

Janice works too. She only does part-time at an estate agent's, but audio typing is demanding on concentration. With all the work at home – cleaning, washing, mending, ironing – Janice too feels stressed at the end of the day. Alistair, Wendy and Anna come in for the worst of it. Except at weekends and on holidays, their parents have got into the you-snap-first-and-I'll-snap-back syndrome.

When Janice and Ken aren't snapping at each other (a level of conflict they seem to have got used to), they are snappy at the three children. This usually involves demands of various kinds.

'You're not going up to your room till you've washed up the supper things.'

'No you're not going out to the cinema tonight. Your mother needs help with the washing.'

'Over my dead body, young man. I don't care whether you have got the money. Mopeds are dangerous. And if I can walk to work, you can walk to school.'

There are ways of communicating perfectly reasonable requests and views which win acceptance, and others which create conflict. The transition from child to adult is a sensitive matter to handle on both sides. Just because a child may lack wisdom and finesse does not mean that he or she lacks either intelligence or sensibility. Parents have no right to demand servile obedience from their children. 'You do this. You do that.' There has to be some kind of learning principle behind what they are asking. In their turn, children have no right to neglect their responsibility to co-operate willingly with what their parents ask of them. It is back to first principles again. The purpose which lies behind the call to obedience is of first importance.

Wait till you're my age

Richard, a man in his late thirties, spoke of an argument he had with his mother at about the age of sixteen. Richard's mother thought it unreasonable that he had stayed out all night at a party. He had not told his parents where he was. He thought his mother was being unreasonable in complaining about it. But he commented that he has never forgotten what she said. While Richard was fuming away, his mother calmly informed him that he would probably only understand when he had children of his own. She advised him that parents sometimes do know best, and to ensure the best they sometimes have to insist that children do as they say.

Richard records that he always found the advice, 'You'll understand when you are grown up' really infuriating. But the reason for the discussion was that recently, he had found it to be true. He has only come to appreciate properly the importance of loving discipline and the need for obedience since he and Maggie have had children themselves. Their two boys of three and five would be eating Jaffa cakes for breakfast, lunch and supper if their parents didn't insist that they eat up most of what is put in front of them. They have to learn.

Scream and shout

Those who have never lived through it can hardly imagine the fuss that little children can make if they do not get their own way. Fights, tears, screams and shouts. All over biscuits! Richard and Maggie love them dearly, but sometimes discipline is necessary otherwise nothing would be learned. The arguments are a way of reinforcing the necessity for obedience. Without the imperative of obedience, albeit lovingly enforced, the child may come to conclude that if he holds out for long enough, demanding his own will, he'll get his own way in the end. That is a sure way to develop an adult with a strongly manipulative personality, which can arouse devastatingly negative reactions in the lives of others when the child comes of age.

Stop and think

Let's pause for a moment and think about this issue of arguments and the learning process. If you have children, of whatever age, ask these questions of yourself and your partner.

- What kinds of argument do you have with your children? Do they cover any repeated areas of concern?
- Do you have arguments which are largely the result of a clash of views, or do you use arguments to clarify actions or values?
- How often do your arguments contribute to the learning process, or how much are they destructive?
- How steamed up do you get, and why?

We'll come to a strategy for coping with these differences in a moment. But if we want to adopt an approach to family life which is Christ-centred in its essence, we must ask how we are to glorify God in the relationship of parents to children and children to parents.

The command

A clue is contained in Paul's command, 'Children, obey your parents, in the Lord', which is bracketed with the quotation of the fifth commandment, 'Honour your father and mother' (Eph. 6:1–2).

In these words, Paul turns from the principle of the learning process to the command to glorify God in our relationships. Obedience is now seen as part of our responsibility to God himself. Paul says we are to obey our parents 'in the Lord'. And we are to honour our father and mother.

Hindu disciple

An Indian boy of Hindu parents was strongly influenced by Christian friends and himself became a committed follower of Christ. His parents, who were fair and liberal-minded people, were nonetheless confused and upset, and while giving Rajiv freedom to follow his convictions, they forbade him to be baptised until he had come of age. This caused Rajiv a great deal of turmoil, particularly as others of his friends had been baptised by immersion in the local Baptist church.

An important change took place in Rajiv's experience. Someone brought to his notice the fifth commandment, to honour your father and mother. After thought and prayer about its implications, Rajiv decided to co-operate and submitted to his parents' wishes. Rajiv was nearing adulthood. As it turned out, this act of obedience became a powerful witness to his parents of his transformed character clearly emerging since making his commitment to Christ. When he eventually turned eighteen his father told him he had no further objection to his being baptised, a decision based more on Rajiv's co-operative attitude a year before than on his recent coming of age.

The impact of obedience

There is a principle here for children and teenagers who live in non-Christian homes. Obedience to parents can be a powerful witness to the reality of life in Christ. God still requires obedience to parents even if they are not Christians. The principle 'obey your parents . . . for this is right' is drawn from creation; it applies to all people, Christian or not. That being so, are there circumstances where you have to draw the line?

Rajiv, the seventeen-year-old Hindu boy, was right when he decided his baptism could wait. In any case, he knew that when he came of age he would be able to obey God's commandment to be baptised. But what if his parents had forbidden him to pray and read his Bible? Then the command to obey his parents 'in the Lord' would set a different limit on that obedience. His baptism could wait. But he couldn't deny Christ by ignoring his basic relationship with him.

Anything that will ultimately be displeasing to God is included in the idea of 'obeying in the Lord'. Because 'obedience in the Lord' reminds us we have a higher allegiance than that of purely human dimension. This can apply to moral issues and anything which runs counter to the Bible's teaching. God holds us responsible for our actions.

Unreasonable demands

How should we counsel young people to respond when a parent seems unreasonable in a particular demand or request?

Jamie, a bright, outgoing sixteen-year-old member of a church youth group, was planning to go to its meeting following the Sunday evening service. When his mother heard that the subject was sex before marriage, she refused to let him attend. His mother clearly did not approve of the subject as being suitable for a teenager of Jamie's age! It is obviously very frustrating when something like this happens. It could just as easily have been a refused request to come home late or stay the night at a friend's house. When you are at this age and you come up against a brick wall, you do sometimes feel like screaming with frustration.

But Jamie's attitude in this case was right. He was prepared, even though reluctantly, to do what his mother required. No parent is perfect. Even when parents get it wrong, Paul's point is that if you are Christian, your obedience is in the Lord. And that emphasis and focus release you. When you obey, you are honouring God by what you do.

So when counselling young people on this point we have to say that providing it is not contradictory to God's will, 'be obedient'. Not because your parents are right, but because your obedience is to Christ; your obedience is in the Lord and you are therefore honouring God by so

FAMILY RELATIONSHIPS

doing. But obedience is not the same as servility. The motivation for the call to obedience is not always easy to discern. But where servility and not obedience is called for, then the command to obey clearly does not apply. When the relationship of parents and children is at this low ebb, mutual love and respect need careful maintenance and rebuilding, for the principle of honouring one another contributes importantly to love, trust and self-worth.

Giving honour

There is a double emphasis on honouring in Paul's teaching, for the fifth commandment itself, 'Honour your father and mother', contains the emphasis on honouring parents. To honour someone means openly to acknowledge their worth. Have you noticed how often when relationships go wrong we are focusing on people's weaknesses and not on their worth at all?

There seem to be two ways of focusing on someone's weaknesses. One is in your mind, by what you consistently let yourself think about someone. The other is by what you say, either to them directly or behind their backs. Honouring someone, by contrast, means putting their weaknesses on one side. So, however young or old we may be, there is an important implication contained in the commandment. To honour our parents is not an option, it is a commandment from God.

- At whatever age, whether your parents are alive or dead, do you regularly think or speak negatively about them? Has this become a habit of mind?
- What are your first dominant thoughts on contemplating your father or mother?
- Why do you think in this way? In the light of the fifth commandment should you be modifying your response in some way?

Think about your reaction to these questions and pause for a moment, before you continue reading, to assess your response.

The promise

The issue behind these questions becomes clearer when Paul speaks of what is promised to us. He has spoken of the principle and the command. Here is the promise: 'Honour your father and mother that it may go well with you, and that you may enjoy long life on the earth.'

- Ask yourself if within you there is any resentment to one or both of your parents in some significant way.
- Do you see that the promise of things going well with us is attached to keeping the commandment to honour our parents?

Many people who seek professional help for problems of depression, anxiety, stress, relationship difficulties and related issues have discovered the importance of problems they have experienced in connection with their parents. But so often, though the parents may have done stupid and unwise things, the problem lies with the *reaction* of the child. It is possible to let resentment and hurt linger on for years, when it should have been released long before.

Forgiving father

Joyce, a lady now in her forties, had a father who consistently underappreciated her. She can't remember ever being shown any affection as a child. He died ten years ago. Yet she still finds herself full of frustration and anger towards him. She feels deeply rejected by a man who was in fact very shy, and apparently found it extremely hard to express himself affectionately. It is only after a long period of counselling that she has at last realised that she has to drop her charge against her father, and to forgive him for not being the person that she longed he should be.

The years of resentment had caused a great deal of inner pain. Joyce has now learned to honour her father's memory and to see his worth. As a result, she is no longer frustrated or angry deep within herself.

Honouring someone does not mean turning a blind eye to weakness. It means putting weakness on one side, and openly acknowledging the positive worth of the person. Not ignoring the bad side, but dwelling positively on the good side.

Reassessing attitudes

If you have realised that you resent a parent, living or dead, in some significant way, will you reassess your attitude towards them? You may have good grounds for your negative feelings, but those feelings will not do you any good. In fact they can well do you harm. Bitterness, anger and resentment can act as emotional cancers, eating us up inside.

And there is another angle. Some of us have to learn to forgive our parents for not being the people we might have wanted them to be. We have to drop the charge and put the painful memories on one side. The honouring of our parents through our attitudes and actions plays an enormously important part towards our mental and spiritual health. This is a God-inspired principle. It has been rediscovered by dynamic psychology in the twentieth century, but it is an ancient insight and has been in the Bible all along. 'Honour your father and mother that it may go well with you, and that you may enjoy long life on the earth.'

Stop goading them

Paul's direction to parents is contained in the words, 'Fathers, do not exasperate your children; instead, bring them up in the training and instruction of the Lord' (Eph. 6:4). The words apply to fathers *and* mothers because the context and the Greek original text both suggest this interpretation. The New English Bible recognises this. 'Parents, don't goad your children into resentment.' Paul is recognising the sensitive nature of children themselves and of family relationships as a whole.

Checkpoints

So what should we do when the balloon goes up? How should you respond when there are squabbles and arguments; when you want your own way and no one wants to give it to you? Here are some guidelines, derived from the New Testament's teaching on these matters (cf. Eph. 6:1–4; Col. 3:20–4; Titus 2:1–8).

- Parents should not have wrong expectations of their children.

The expression of wrong expectations is the cause of an immense amount of anger and frustration in the lives of children of whatever age. It is so important to accept people as they are.

- Beware of your own frustrated ambitions.

FAMILY RELATIONSHIPS

Frustrated ambitions can contribute to wrong expectations and fuel the fire of anger and resentment. It is selfish to try and live out your frustrated ambitions through the life of your child. It is cruel. And when your children fail to live up to the hopes you have for them, you imply they are not acceptable people in their own right. Negative expectations, often expressed by comparisons of one child with another, get under the skin and stay there. They irritate, inflame and sometimes explode with pained and affronted venom. Wrong expectations from parents lead to enormous frustration. Argumentative families thrive on them.

- Beware of projecting untrue parental images.

Parents are not omnicompetent, and it is important that children know this. When our daughter Rebecca was three she came to see me in my office one day and said, 'Daddy, you're the leader of the church, and you know *everything*.' It was a charming comment. She is older and wiser now. It is important that Christian parents are honest, open and real to their children. Let's be honest about our failings. That doesn't mean we have to tell children every little embarrassing detail about ourselves. It does mean not hiding things which are important in the life of a family. It is vital that children know that their parents make mistakes and are just as much in need of God's forgiveness as they are. Equally, it is also important for parents to apologise to their children when they have wronged or harmed them in some way. Without this experience of reconciliation in the home there is little chance to learn models of mutual forgiveness and the reinstatement of love.

- Do make the effort to encourage openness in your family.

Children can help parents in this respect. Sometimes children need to break the conspiracy of silence. Maybe there is a marriage problem, for many otherwise healthy marriages have their ups and downs, and many others run into serious trouble.

- Sometimes even little children can help resolve problems when they are explained openly and simply. Children can sense when things are wrong. Many private problems need airing in the family.

Not all marriage problems can be aired by any means, and some are best resolved privately. To involve children in levels of conflict they cannot understand can be upsetting and bewildering for them. It may be far better to have an open argument than a family where no one tells the truth about how they really feel. Encourage openness, and you'll encourage emotional and spiritual health as well.

The family conference

In a fast-moving world, family members may be so busy that they hardly see one another individually, let alone together, from one week to the next. Those who believe that the family is a major force for good in our society should strive to move against this social trend. For when there is little actual communication, barriers soon go up, and with them come misunderstandings, conflict and anger.

The family conference is a valuable strategy for coping with family conflict. It encourages open communication, and learning about processes of living in mutually beneficial ways. A family conference is a regular get-together where issues needing attention can be sympathetically dealt with, and given time, attention and constructive understanding. Family conferences are best conducted in as natural a manner as possible. If they take place from the children's earliest years, they'll be seen as a natural resource in family interactions. When appropriate, members of the family can pray for each other, not as a matter of form, but as a genuine response to Christ's centrality and reality in the life of the family.

Every family needs to find its own best time or times. There are no rules about this. It is simply a matter of maintaining communication in the family unit. A meal when everybody can be present is a good time for such a family talk and get-together. Some families with otherwise complex patterns of activity make an effort that everybody should be present to gather at breakfast time, say. Like a marriage, the important matter is to be talking and remain talking. The 'conference' is the sympathetic review of family plans, objectives, differences of opinion, and any issues which might be ready to emerge full blown into a conflict. Sometimes this happens spontaneously and regularly in a family without the need for extra organisation. Otherwise such times can be worked out in advance and become a first call on everyone's schedule.

When families talk in this way, a number of different benefits accrue.

- Children learn how to take part in discussion, not just in the making of statements.
- The child's contribution is recognised as being valid and worth while. A child can be encouraged to express feelings in words, and his or her constructive contributions are recognised and appreciated.
- This is a valuable arena for a child to experience the defeat of a cherished idea. Explanation can be given, recompense can be paid. It teaches a child to let go of his own will for the sake of others, with whom he has to live and let live.

- A child may have right, misunderstood, or as yet unheard of ideas for his parents and siblings to listen to. These open family meetings provide a focus for debating your own view, while learning to listen and give way to others.
- Families which function well together need to take time with each other. Conflicts themselves take time to unravel and require the investment of a great deal of commitment and effort. Such an awareness is, as it is designed to be, a training for life itself. Training within the home in an informal 'conference' situation greatly benefits the development of the awareness that time to listen is one of the greatest gifts we give to those we love.
- Such meetings provide the experience of security within the family. When topics of concern at all levels are being regularly opened up, there will be a consistency of treatment for all. The family as a whole cares about the decisions made and the matters discussed. The fact of meeting together emphasises the commitment of the family *to* the family and to the individuals within it.

Reconciliation

As you have been reading these thoughts, have you come to the decision that you need to be reconciled to members of your family? Parents to children, child to parents, brothers or sisters; whatever the relationship may be, do you need to be reconciled? Do you need to say sorry? Do you need to change your attitudes, your thoughts or behaviour?

Snappy families, like all other families, need to grow in love. Love means learning to accept one another. It means thinking before you speak, trying hard not to get all steamed up and confrontational. It means talking things through. It means not being too proud to admit you are in the wrong. That is the way forward for snappy families.

It is a learning process. It is not just children who are learners, it is parents too. And families need to help each other because, in the end, it's all about learning to love.

- Do you need to be reconciled?
- Should you be acting as the peacemaker in your family, or the one who breaks the conspiracy of silence?
- A personal conversation, a telephone call or a letter may be all that is necessary to break the ice and start the work of reconciliation.
- If there's something needing to be said, don't shirk it. You owe it to your family, and to God.
- Spend some moments in quiet, look back over the pages of this chapter, reconsidering what you have learned and the thoughts which have come to you.
- Bring your thoughts to God in prayer, and then take any action necessary.

5

WORK RELATIONSHIPS

Work relationships are often perceived in terms of conflict. Yet there is nothing inherent in the *nature* of work to produce such responses. We bring to our working relationships the same potential for disordered conduct as we bring to any other area of our lives. Conflict is common to all human situations. It is as natural to find conflict present in the work environment as it is in the family, marriage, or any other human context.

Lead stories

While recognising that conflict is something we *bring* to a relationship and is not *inherent* in the substance of the relationship itself, the *circumstances* of those relationships can nonetheless bring enormous pressure to bear on the responses we may make. In all industrialised nations such strained relationships are no more publicly evident than in the regular conflicts between workforce and management, where poor industrial relations are so often manifested in disputes and strikes.

Bitter accusations, unwillingness to listen, disregard for justice, the breakdown of negotiations, the withdrawal of labour – all these are issues of continual attention and fervent debate for politicians, journalists, and public alike, and regular copy for lead stories for the media. Only the names of the participants in these daily dramas need be changed. The wearying scenario of disregard for human sensitivity, industrial rights and the need for consultation, endlessly repeats itself with disappointing and frustrating frequency.

Ethical imperative

We have already established that conflict is best handled not by clever tips for healthy friendships, but by self-understanding, well-practised interpersonal skills for listening and the resolving of differences, and the careful application of God's principles for the specific areas of life and experience in which we find ourselves. Our need to look more closely at the working relationship is not that strife and strikes are an issue of constant interest, nor that work conflicts are part of the distressing experience of vast numbers. The effort to apply our faith in Christ to our working situations, with the many practical and ethical difficulties implied by such a concern, is part of our overall responsibility to God. The command that Christians should be salt and light in whatever aspect of society they function (Matt. 5:13–14) is part of God's general strategy in the world, and the responsibility, therefore, of all Christians.

Gospel images

The salt-light picture used by Jesus was immediately clear to his followers of the first-century world. To be engaged in the same strategy, we need to be clear that we have fully entered into this same understanding. Salt was used in Jesus's day both for flavouring and preserving. The implication is clear: Jesus's followers are to stem the tide of godlessness and prevent the sourness of decay in practical ways in the working world. Christians should show forth the light of the transforming power of the gospel in their lives.

Transformed living

Such considerations should bring encouragement to anyone concerned for the cause of Christ. Any serious attempt at Christian living, however small in scope, makes an important contribution to the overall effect and impact of the salt and light strategy envisaged by Jesus. Whether we work in the public or private sectors, or are self-employed; whether we work as operators, managers, supervisors or directors; whatever our field, the effective application of faith to work can be a challenging, stretching and sometimes frustrating task. The stakes, however, are high. Given that so many of our waking hours are spent working, this is where the task of establishing the ethical claims of God's kingdom are most needed.

Storm tactics

Janice is a primary school teacher in North London. St Matthew's School has gone through a difficult patch in the last few years. It is surprising how quickly rumours spread. But rumours are all they were. There was a general feeling among the local community a few years ago that academic standards at the school had slipped, and many parents opted for other schools in the area for their children. This left St Matthew's with a reduced pupil–teacher ratio, which in time led to staff cuts and lower funding.

A new head teacher has made much difference in the last two years and the school is beginning to pick up in many ways. However, all the teachers have been working under strained conditions and many are tired and overworked. Stress is quite a problem among the teaching staff since they are still overstretched, and it takes very little extra pressure to produce a minor crisis.

Such a crisis happened in the stormy weather of a particularly difficult week in February, when everyone was feeling just a little touchy. All the additional effort to repair wind damage, and coping with the extra demands of old buildings in poor weather, didn't help to relieve the pressures, especially as some of the boys had been rather overexcited and badly behaved. Many of the teachers feel that firmer discipline is needed in the school, although the head has a freer approach not always shared by Janice and some of her colleagues. But when Janice put her convictions into practice, she was shocked at the response.

Janice believes that children should know when they are going beyond what is acceptable and that a clear framework of conduct is necessary for a child's proper development. Eight-year-old Peter comes from a home where he receives very little discipline. He is a pleasant child, but often rowdy, disobedient and rough with others. One Tuesday Janice noticed that Peter had been pushing and shoving Laura during singing. When Laura complained at breaktime that Peter had done the same again, pushing her towards the broken tiles which had recently been blown off the junior hall roof, Janice felt that Peter needed to be shown that what he had done was dangerous and unacceptable. Peter received some firm words and was made to stay inside during breaktime for the next day. On the Wednesday morning, Peter's father sought out Janice. He felt that the discipline was cruel and unnecessary. He said so in no uncertain terms.

Peter's father complained to the head teacher, who quite surprisingly immediately took the parent's side. As it happens, Peter's mother is a governor at the school, although this should have had nothing to do with the matter. However, there had been a number of complaints from parents about the increasingly firm discipline in the school. The rumours had begun to spread, and the truth had been distorted. Janice was to be made a scapegoat. Her head teacher preferred to keep the parents happy, and keep the numbers up. It was an act of pure convenience to tell Peter's father that his son had been treated insensitively and perhaps unjustly. It was an easy way of keeping a potentially difficult parent quiet. As a result, Janice was wrongly accused of victimisation and excessive punishment.

How things blow up. Janice herself received a few firm words. She was amazed and hurt. All this when her only motivation was to go the extra mile under all circumstances. The staff were all under pressure. This was the wrong time for a confrontation. Janice felt like chucking it all in there and then. When you are stretched, it doesn't take much to snap you apart. Janice was certainly helped by the sympathetic understanding of her fellow teachers, but the fact that she stayed and weathered the storm had much to do with her deeply held conviction that work must be seen as service. Janice believed that misunderstanding or mistreatment in themselves, though undesirable, should not necessarily deflect you from your course.

Working principles

The principles which underlie the working relationship are as important for our understanding and behaviour at work, as the principles which underlie any other area of life. Janice might have quit but for her strong conviction, as a Christian, that the service element is a high part of the calling for anyone in employment. It is not surprising that the New Testament has important principles to offer concerning working relationships. One place where these principles find expression in their most cogent form is in Paul's letter to the Colossians. In the practically orientated conclusion of the letter, Paul's directives are highly relevant, touching on principles of mutual conduct, controversy, and our need for fulfilment and satisfaction in what we do.

Paul at Colossae

> Slaves, obey your earthly masters in everything; and do it, not only when their eye is on you and to win their favour, but with sincerity of heart, and reverence for the Lord. Whatever you do, work at it with all your heart, as working for the Lord, not for men, since you know that you will receive an inheritance from the Lord as a reward. It is the Lord Christ you are serving. Anyone who does wrong will be repaid for his wrong, and there is no favouritism. Masters, provide your slaves with what is right and fair, because you know you also have a Master in heaven (Col. 3:22–4:1).

A superficial reading of this passage might suggest little practical relevance for present-day dealings in employment situations. The talk of slaves and masters sounds out of date, an anachronism in relation to conflicts experienced today. The subject of Paul's directive also raises questions of moral acceptability. Does the Bible condone or even promote slavery? If it does, that only reinforces the irrelevance of Biblical teaching to the relationships of workers and bosses today.

If this passage does have central and significant relevance to contemporary working relationships, we must begin by clarifying in what ways the issues touched upon by Paul's words address themselves to current situations and concerns. We need to be sure of the relevance of the circumstances Paul is describing if we are to seek to apply his principles to our lives now.

The Colossian heresy

As a letter, Colossians is a response by Paul to an actual living situation. Paul never explicitly describes the heresy he seeks to expose at Colossae, though from his statement it is possible to piece together the evidence of what had been such a destructive influence. As Paul writes to this leading city in Asia Minor (present-day Turkey) around the year AD 60 he makes many statements in opposition to the false teachers whose influence has apparently been so prevalent. In particular, it appears there was a specific leader at Colossae who had come to a position of authority. His understanding of Christ and Christianity had become badly distorted through a kind of super-spirituality. This may have been characterised by a mystic other-worldliness which had little time for the concerns of this world, and the working out of faith in relation to the everyday challenges of life.

For Paul the issue which dominates the whole letter is one of the truth of the gospel, and its consequent implications for practical Christian living. He responds to the Colossian heresy by spending exactly half his letter reminding the Colossians just how magnificent, supreme and totally adequate for every aspect of life Jesus Christ truly is. And then, with his foundations once more rightly in place, he continues in the second half of his letter to spell out the specific relevance of faith in Christ for daily living, particularly in this arena of relationships.

The Lord of life

So in the second part of the letter (from Col. 3:18 ff.) Jesus is seen not only as Lord of the world, but also as Lord of all human relationships. He is Lord of family life – for husbands, wives, children and their parents. Then as we shall see (from Col. 3:22–4:1), he is Lord of the working environment, the true basis of all working relationships for those who are committed to him. It is important to understand this context of Paul's teaching, for a deep understanding of the adequacy of Christ is the setting in which these relationships are meant to function and grow. This is the foundation for a true theology of the working relationship, without which there are no practical principles to which Christians can appeal to make their approach to work (and its conflicts and difficulties) any different from the non-Christian world.

Slaves and masters

Slaves and masters were the workers and bosses throughout the Greek-speaking world of the first century. The relationship between these two groups defines the working environment to which Paul is referring. Before we establish that it is proper to equate slaves and masters with the association between employee and employer today, an important question of Biblical background and ethics needs to be addressed.

Status quo theology?

By these words (and the similar statements of Eph. 6:5–9) isn't Paul condoning slavery? Doesn't he seem to be content with the status quo? Isn't he rather lax in calling for social change? Could the implication be that today the Christian at work is quietly to put up with any kind of abuse or ill-treatment? Should Janice suffer in silence in the face of continued unfair treatment by her head? Is it a modern myth that workers have rights – a wicked concoction of trade unions? When Paul says 'slaves obey your earthly masters in everything', is he not in fact reinforcing the outrage of social divisions for many centuries to come? Isn't Paul himself, more than any other, responsible for the scornful words of Karl Marx, that religion is the opium of the people?

Contextual thinking

These are reasonable questions, but the answer in each case has to be 'no'. As ever, context is important, particularly the wider context of New Testament teaching. The words of Jesus help to illuminate the theology of Paul, especially when the context of Paul's words is taken seriously into account. Jesus said, 'I have come that they may have life and have it to the full' (John 10:10). Just before his words on slaves and masters, Paul refers to this abundant life which in itself is a central gift of the gospel. 'Here there is no Greek or Jew, circumcised or uncircumcised, barbarian, Scythian, slave, or free, but Christ is all, and is in all' (Col. 3:11). That is a revolutionary truth, and far more revolutionary than that of which Karl Marx ever dreamed. Paul declares that a freedom from the old inequalities, those divisions in society which have alienated man from man in a whole variety of ways, is available now through the gospel. In experience it will be a growing reality. But since those divisions are abolished in Christ, in experience we must aim to abolish them in practice. This is the basis of Paul's theology of the social freedom inherent in the gospel.

Theological practice

It is true that Paul could not preach that freedom without fairly being asked how the theology works out in practice, especially where the inequalities of society, at least on the surface of things, remain unchanged. The nature of the times sheds important light on this. It would have been humanly impossible for the early Christians to alter the economic base of the whole Roman Empire. To expect Paul to call for the abolition of slavery at this point in time is to be guilty of unhistorical thinking. Yet with all this taken into account, as both the little letter to Philemon and the teaching found in Colossians and Ephesians show, Paul's theology of work *was* highly radical. It was *so* radical that in later centuries it did lead to the abolition of slavery in the Western world.

Whatever our working situation, whether we view ourselves as being in a position of unique privilege or even perhaps severe disadvantage, Paul has something fundamental and life-changing to say to us in terms of principle and practical application.

A dual relationship

Maybe you are absolutely bored to pieces at work. Are you like Oscar Wilde, who said, 'I love work, I can sit and look at it for hours'? Perhaps you're the boss they love to hate. Maybe you do an ordinary job, and you wonder how to do it as a Christian? Perhaps you experience conflict with other workers, or are working in a variety of situations seeking to bring peace where there is strife. However you fit in, Paul enunciates one fundamental principle which characterises all other aspects of working relationships and practice. The principle involves what it means to be a follower of Christ, for as a Christian all your relationships relate as much to God as to men.

This dual relationship is the principle and key to all Paul's teaching on work. Paul is careful to emphasise that relationships relate both to God and man by the statement which comes immediately prior to, and also introduces, his section on the full range of relationships in which Christians will be involved. 'Whatever you do, whether in word or deed, do it all in the name of the Lord Jesus' (Col. 3:17). This implies there is not one single corner of our lives in which Jesus does not have an interest. As Christians, our lives are to be seen primarily as service offered to the Lord. That must mean that whatever we are involved in is conditioned by one overall fact: whatever we do is either to the service or *dis*service of Christ.

There is a parallel with actors in a play. Actors don't just exist to please themselves, to have a good time, to act as they choose, either well or badly. They exist to please the audience looking on. It is the audience for which they and the play exist; that is their whole reason for being. And, put simply, followers of Christ exist for Christ, to please him, as he 'looks on'; for whatever we do in word or deed, we are to do for the honour of Jesus Christ the Lord.

Workers and bosses

Paul provides two directives. Our way now should be clear to accepting the propriety of applying these principles to the modern-day working environment, calling the slaves, workers and the masters, bosses. The workers provide the largest group, and the first directive is addressed to them.

Service of Christ

A Christian is in the Lord's service. 'Whatever you do, work at it with all your heart, as working for the Lord, not for men' (Col. 3:23). I don't know how a first-century slave would have taken this directive to regard work as service to Christ; but I can imagine some twentieth-century slaves thinking such sentiments run sharply against the grain. Is Paul saying, now you are a Christian, you may be in a dead-end job, but you'd better grin and bear it? Is Paul just spiritualising the everyday drudgery? Can't we smell the opiate of the people again? Is this his way of keeping the masses down by spiritualising their lot?

Dead-end job

Jack is a plant manager. In his case, that's an up-market name for a caretaker. He does more than an ordinary caretaker would do at the small plastics company where he has worked for years. But Jack is bored with what he does. At his age, and where he lives, he doesn't really have much hope of getting anything more advanced, though he is certainly intelligent and able. The trouble is, he lets his frustration get the better of him sometimes and snarls and snaps at anyone who is not too much in authority over him. For the last year or so he's gained a reputation as 'Jack the sniper'. He hasn't told anyone how frustrated he is. But the conflicts he generates have much to do with his job dissatisfaction. Jack has often wondered how the

Bible can really say, 'Whatever you do, work at it with all your heart, as working for the Lord, not for men.' Jack knows his heart is not in it. He's relieved he can pay his bills and keep body and soul reasonably well together, but that's as far as it goes.

Two-level challenge

It is surprising how much energy it is possible to use up in inner conflicts. That feeling that you are not where you are meant to be. Sometimes that inner frustration is an important precursor for change. Other times it can indicate a lack of understanding and acceptance of this important spiritual principle. A Christian is in the Lord's service. It would be easy to caricature Paul's teaching on work, but what he is doing is to challenge at two levels. He wants Christ to be brought clearly into the picture of working matters, not for Christians in the working world to secularise their task so that Christ is absent from their thinking. So the two levels he proposes are what we do and what we feel about what we do. We might describe these, therefore, as the issues of performance and job satisfaction.

Performance – go for quality

'Slaves, obey your earthly masters in everything. And do it not only when their eye is on you and to win their favour, but with sincerity of heart and reverence for the Lord' (Col. 3:22).

The word 'obey' settles unpleasantly and suspiciously on twentieth-century ears, but Paul means by it what it says. Many aspects of twentieth-century living have made us distrustful of authority, and when authority is abused that is understandable. Nevertheless, by 'obey' Paul is not referring to servile obedience to an authoritarian master, but an injunction to workers to carry out the job an employer has for them to accomplish. Paul means that workers should do in practice what the employer requires. He is saying go for quality, do a good job, and be aware of the presence or absence of an underlying spiritual motivation.

Extra care

If you want to hear complaints about service industries, the quality of garage maintenance is a regular target for consumer watchdogs and grousers. However, when our car was serviced at a small back-street garage which we had never tried before, what really impressed us was not only the mechanical quality of the service, but the extra care taken. Someone had take the trouble to remove all the children's sweet papers from the ashtray, and clean underneath the mats as well. It doesn't usually happen. It was more than was strictly required. But this is exactly the kind of quality of which Paul is speaking.

You just seem to do the job well while the boss's eye is on you, but you don't really care about genuine quality in what you do. According to Paul, you are functioning in a substandard Christian way. Our Christian motivation is to honour Christ in all we do, including the quality of our work irrespective of whom we work for, whether they are good employers or not.

In a sense, there is a resemblance here to doing something like dusting. Some people do the bare minimum, just the surface that shows. But when you dust behind and underneath, as well as on the surface, then you are taking both care and the right kind of pride in what you are doing. That kind of thoroughness can be given in service to Jesus.

Working standards

Going for quality not only means the way we do our work, but the standards with which we conduct ourselves at work.

- Are you sure your boss doesn't mind your using the telephone for personal calls?
- Should you really be using the photocopier for your own use?
- What about letting your lunch hour run on so often?
- Should you be more diligent in the way you apply yourself to the tasks in hand?
- What are the issues which affect the standards of your witness to Christ at work?
- What other standards should you be vigilant about?

Christ does care about the details of how we conduct ourselves in all these situations, because the standards we have at work either honour him or dishonour him. The emphasis of Paul is clear, we are to go for quality both in our performance and in the way we conduct ourselves in the workplace. Our service is first to Christ, not to man.

Job satisfaction – work wholeheartedly

What we do is important in its own right, but what we *feel* about what we do is also critical. Our feelings so often determine how well or otherwise we shall choose to perform, and will also affect the quality of our work relationships. 'Whatever you do, work at it with all your heart, as working for the Lord, not for men' (Col. 3:23).

There is much discussion in all quarters on the importance of job satisfaction. Many people regard job satisfaction as getting the formula right. Matching our gifts and preferences to the job and its opportunities. 'A man

WORK RELATIONSHIPS

can do nothing better than to ... find satisfaction in his work' (Eccles. 2:24). However true that may be, many people don't have that privilege today, but have to face repetitive, uninteresting patterns of employment. So when Paul issues the principle, 'work ... with all your heart as working for the Lord' what does he actually mean, and how does it relate to those in this category?

Paul's major concern must be the consequence of being delivered from drudgery.

- What are the most enjoyable aspects of your work?
- What aspects of your work do you really dislike?
- What are the most stimulating elements of what you do?
- Are there certain elements you find intolerably dull and boring?
- What effect do the more negative aspects of your work have on you and your relationships with others?

Boredom and drudgery

Many people hate certain aspects of their work. Even the most interesting of jobs will have its fair share of dull moments, for there is drudgery in every job. Are you one of those in a completely dead-end job? Are you frustrated by the dull monotony and lack of prospects?

Being bored and frustrated is a problem for many people; even for those with positions of responsibility and influence, there can be a lot of drudgery involved. Yet we need at this point to take in deeply what Paul is indicating. He is saying our true master is in heaven. Part of our difficulty with concepts like this is that we are quite used to being told we are servants of Christ. Perhaps a fresher way of seeing the truth here is to turn the whole statement around. So it then says, Christ is our employer. We can be proud to work for him. Dick Lucas comments: 'Such is our work and dignity in Christ, that any task undertaken for our master, however menial, is fit to be part of our service to the Lord of glory' *(The Message of Colossians*, IVP 1984).

Rethink

Can you learn to think of yourself and your work in this way? It is powerful when you do. It is the secret of peace and contentment. That is why one of the greatest minds of the ancient world, the Apostle Paul himself, could find contentment in sewing tents for a living. And yet he went to some lengths to press home the validity of this attitude. 'I have learned to be content whatever the circumstances' (Phil. 4:11).

Learning to be content is the great secret of life, for every aspect of our jobs, however boring, can become fulfilling when we work at them wholeheartedly, as serving Christ. But simplistic claims have to be swept aside. It means a revolution in our attitudes.

- What real difference will it make to you to rethink this aspect of your employment?
- What effect will it have on any strain you are experiencing in any of your relationships?

Pressure points

Stress and conflict belong together, and the way we feel about what we do makes a great deal of difference to our inner store of pressures. When the pot begins to boil and the bubbles rise quickly to the surface, it doesn't take much to make it boil right over. Our emotional temperature can so easily make itself felt to others. We may be cross and short for no other reason than that we are frustrated and dissatisfied. Inner striving and resentment at what we do has no solution unless we move on to something else, or change our attitude. And the changing of attitude, important as it is when staying where you are, is also just as important if God is going to move you on to something new. The motivation must be right if we are to be effective in the Lord's service.

Of course, there's no point in doing something intrinsically dull just for the sake of it. But Paul is claiming that attitudes are everything, and ongoing dissatisfaction can be a very ungodly outlook. Christians are under obligation to be constantly watchful on this point. We are not employed just for work – dull, boring, monotonous work. We are employed for service, wholehearted service to Christ; and the world needs to see it, to realise that Christians are different because of who our Lord is.

Fair deals

Injustice at work is one of the prime sources of conflict, especially in annual pay rounds, but also in many other ways. Paul's teaching has sometimes been unfairly caricatured as being on the bosses' side. But in no sense can that be true. Paul makes it clear that there is no partiality when it comes to God's judgment on the employee or the employer. 'Anyone who does wrong will be repaid for his wrong and there is no favouritism' (Col. 3:25). He tells the employers to 'provide your slaves with what is right and fair, because you know that you also have a Master in Heaven' (Col. 4:1).

Slave rights

To recognise the full force of this injunction, we must remember that the slave in those days had no rights. The slave was nothing in the eyes of the law. He had no right to marry or to father children. When he was past work, he was thrown out to die. He certainly had nothing even resembling pension rights. Paul's teaching must have come with all the more force to his original hearers. There were no trades unions in those days, and there was no recourse to justice in any form. Yet here it is said, the slave must be freely given what he cannot claim for himself; what no one would even claim for him.

Maybe in Paul's time, given these social conditions, this brief command was even harder to carry out than anything asked of the slaves. You can imagine the kind of impact and consternation Paul's teaching must have made. Slave owners who became Christians revolutionised their treatment of slaves, giving to them the justice and the fair treatment that hitherto had been unknown in the ancient world.

Them and us

That being so, how much more should Christian employers work for justice and the fair treatment of their workforce. So often in working relationships there is a them and us mentality. The management versus the unions. A confrontationalism which we have learned from modern politics. That may be the way the world does its business, but it is not to be the way the Lord's people should do theirs. 'Bear with each other and forgive whatever grievances you may have against one another' (Col. 3:13). This imperative applies to both employers and employees as much as to those Christians at work in a secular context.

It doesn't matter whether you work alongside non-Christians, as most do, or with Christians, as is the experience of a minority. In either situation the above approach is the way Christians should contribute to managing industrial relations.

That's all very well, you may say, but not if you've got a boss like mine, or your office has a filing clerk like ours. That union has cost us thousands with its needless disputes. My supervisor has made my life a misery.

Conflicting interests

So how do we resolve conflicts of interest? The first step is to see things as others do. Try putting yourself into the other person's shoes. You are going to have to work hard at it. Forgiveness and acceptance, and all the other positive attitudes Paul requires and prescribes, are always going to cost you something. The cost of discipleship often fails to be spelt out in Christian teaching. But if anyone said that Christianity wasn't going to cost you anything, they were not telling you the full story.

The truth of Christ is meant to touch our working lives, whatever our situations. Of course we must be concerned for justice, and for where justice is violated. Paul is not asking us to be passive. He is asking us to remember that the wrongdoer will be paid back for the wrong he has done, by someone who is a better judge, someone more in possession of all the facts. Ultimate judgment is from God himself.

- Is there a relationship with an individual or group at work where this principle applies to you?
- What practical action can you take to bring this situation into line with God's standard as described by Paul?

In Christ, our human relationships have a vertical and horizontal focus. All our relationships relate to God as well as operating on a human level. Paul enunciates these two imperatives. Employees, regard your work as service to Christ. Employers, respond to your workers as a servant of Christ.

There is here a true conversion taking place in values, attitudes and motivation. Biblically the word conversion means a turn-round, and that is exactly what we have here. Paul is prescribing a true turn-round in the whole arena of relationships at work. This is what Paul's theology means in practice. The worker is now taken up with his boss's needs. And the boss with the worker's needs.

- If you are employed, is your boss getting the quality of labour he has the right to expect?
- If you are an employer, are your workers getting the reward and the conditions and the treatment they have the right to enjoy?

The worker and the boss, the employee and the employer are *both* to be regarded as servants of Christ. In the truest sense, Jesus Christ is our employer over all, and we are ultimately responsible to him. The Lord will understand our weaknesses. He will forgive our failings. But he will not in the end tolerate injustice and unfair treatment on either side. He calls Christians on all sides of industry, and in any working situation, to bring honour to the name of Christ, to deal with the real and potential conflicts of our relationships by applying the principles of service in all we are and do. That is accomplished by remembering, applying and living by this truth: at work, whatever our standing, we are servants of Christ before we are servants of any earthly master.

6

MARRIAGE RELATIONSHIPS

Like the proverbial horse and carriage, conflict and marriage go together. That is not the way Alma Cogan originally conceived her lyric. But in the lives of many people today love and marriage, though ideals, swiftly give way to conflict, strain, unhappiness and divorce. The figures for marriage and divorce from both sides of the Atlantic support this oft-perceived decline in the quality and longevity of marriages today.

In the latest figures for the United Kingdom, in 1987 398,000 marriages were contracted. Of these, 260,000 were first marriages for both partners; 32 per cent of all marriages for that year represented a remarriage where one or both partners had previously been divorced.

Divorce figures have been growing steadily in the UK since 1971 when the Divorce Reform Act 1969 came into force. They peaked in 1985 when a record 191,000 petitions for divorce were filed. The Matrimonial and Family Proceedings Act of 1984 had a startling impact on the state of new but troubled marriages. The Act allowed couples to petition for divorce after the first anniversary of their marriage, instead of after three years as had been upheld previously. After the immediate impact of this change, the figures for 1987 show a total of 165,000 divorces for England and Wales, a fall of 6 per cent since 1985. Yet this still represents over double the figure of 80,000 which was the divorce rate in 1971. (Source: *Social Trends*, the Central Statistical Office.)

For better or worse

Why is it that marriage should be a relationship of such potential closeness, joy and fulfilment, and yet for so many end up in such unhappiness and hurt? In 1987, 9.3 per cent of those who divorced had only lasted one to two years of marriage; 28.6 per cent of those divorced did so after five to nine years of marriage. Statistics suggest that those whose marriages last beyond this period seem to have learned the secret of how to stay together in a stable relationship. Of those who have been married thirty years or more, only 4.3 per cent divorce.

We shall need to deal with some of the questions raised by the sad and painful fact of marriage breakdown and divorce later in this chapter. For the moment we should merely note the high level of dissatisfaction which the general marriage and divorce figures imply.

Liberal divorce

There was much opposition inside and outside Parliament in 1984 when the law was changed allowing divorce petitions after just one year. At the time, many questioned whether it is really possible to make a marriage work after such a short period. Legislators were clearly concerned for those who had entered marriages where they were being harmed and mistreated by their partners. They wished to provide a way out in case of emergency. Yet the liberal interpretation of divorce laws appears to have led to the alarming trends already observed.

If, as many testify, marriage is the most richly rewarding of relationships, it must also be the most testing, with the greatest potential for conflict and pain. The fact is, the closer you get, the sharper you clash. The build-up of intimacy in marriage has potential both for richness of growth, and a destructive explosion. It all hangs on how we manage the communication process. Like a horse and carriage, love and marriage do go together; but selfishness and self-seeking and the anger generated by violated sensitivities and unmet needs are so often the outer evidence of an increasing inner barrenness. Such barrenness is the inevitable outcome where two people are growing apart and out of love. Nothing more sad and painful can be experienced or witnessed.

Worlds apart

Barry and Helen sat opposite each other. They had sought help from the marriage counsellor a little late in the day. Their marriage had been under strain for some years and they had never been brave enough to admit it to a third party.

Recently matters had come to a head. Barry became involved with another woman. It had happened in a way he never expected. Barry had always frowned on those who had affairs. As a Christian, he knew it wasn't right. But nor was his marriage right.

He and Helen had both felt the tensions for some years now. They'd felt them, expressed them, but never seriously aimed to resolve them. In Barry's view, Helen was the moodiest person on earth. Yes, they had been in love once, that was before they had children. They did not need to have a row for Barry to feel constantly undermined by Helen's attitudes, spoken and unspoken.

You wouldn't think it was possible for a middle-aged department store manager to simply crumple before the withering scowls of his wife. That, as Barry explained to the counsellor, was exactly what Helen did to him. Anyway men have physical needs, he complained. Hadn't Helen kept him at arms' length for months now? Not once had she made any attempt to respond to his initiatives. No, Barry had never meant to get involved with Christine. He knew it was wrong, but it is the first experience of real love and tenderness he has known in years.

'But what about me, Barry? You can't just discard me like an empty cigarette packet. I'm a person, too. It's all right for you. You've dragged me along to all your trade shows and staff socials over the years. You've expected your shirts to be perfect, your home clean, your food prepared, your guests fawned over, a woman to keep your bed warm. But what about me? You never consider whether I have feelings. You've never considered whether I might be bored stiff meeting your work colleagues. You're not interested in the things I like. You never play tennis with me because you say I'm not fast enough. You're never in early enough to have an intelligent conversation. And when you are, you hide yourself in your office or get glued to the video. And quite frankly when we are in bed, I might as well be anybody. You do your thing and roll over. No holding. No warmth. You behave sometimes as though I'm an embarrassment to you. So what can I do? What can I do that makes me into an acceptable human being? I suppose this Christine has everything I don't have. Well, I'll tell you one thing. She hasn't had three children. That makes some difference to your life. That's something you men never seem to understand ...'

Reaping the whirlwind

These kinds of exchange are heart-rending to witness. They happen all too often. Acute marriage conflict occurs to all kinds of people. You don't have to be bad, irresponsible, or wickedly maverick, to have a marriage difficulty, or have to face divorce. Such conflict is not *beyond* our control but, left unattended, it can often *take* control. Then it's like a whirlwind, reaping havoc where peace once reigned.

In the end Barry and Helen did separate and eventually they divorced. Their relationship had become conflict-ridden to the point where each of them was desperately unhappy. The catalogue of hurts which had built up over the years was considerable. There is a kind of laziness or weariness which seeps into troubled marriages. After some periods of discouragement, attempts to put things right and make the effort needed to achieve the kinds of adjustment required for mutual happiness are often postponed, then shelved. The catalogue grows, and without mutually purposeful work to reduce the strain, the weight of accusation and blame increases significantly. In Barry and Helen's case, it wasn't that their problems were insoluble. Their load had increased so profoundly, they could muster neither resolve nor desire to do anything lasting about them.

At least, Barry couldn't. It does, of course, take two to make a marriage and most often two to contribute to a conflict. But final breakdown and divorce can be the initiative of one 'unwilling' partner. Difficulties may be mutually contributed, but the unwilling partner is the one who for whatever reason has passed the point of no return. No desire to mend remains.

Two for change

In all my professional experience of giving support to troubled marriages, I have never met any couple who were not able to make considerable strides forward if *both* were genuinely willing to give attention to the issues underlying their discomfort and conflict and make the changes necessary for health and growth. But where there is resistance to change and unwillingness to mend the troubled relationship on behalf of just one partner, understandably the chances of improvement are meagre, and final breakdown, if not inevitable, is certainly threatened.

- If you are married, how much attention do you and your partner give to managing your conflicts?

- When did you last sit down and talk about priorities for your own relationship?
- Do you know what issues really matter for your partner at present?
- How much time each week do you give to finding out what your partner is thinking and feeling over matters which concern him or her?
- When did you last make a considerable personal adjustment to fit in with some deeply felt need your partner has articulated?
- Have you learned to talk naturally and unembarrassedly about sexual matters, with sensitivity and understanding?

Service schedule

All marriages need their regular running maintenance. No car owner can neglect to check such basic safety features as tyres, brakes, oil and steering. If a car is to remain on the road, basic checks and adjustments need to be made regularly. Marriage maintenance is necessary too. Many people do this naturally. Their effectiveness depends on a number of factors, including personality, sensitivity, their parental and other models of marriage (good and poor), and their understanding and level of commitment to each other. Whether this ongoing maintenance is spontaneous or planned, it will always imply the careful management of conflict. For conflict in marriage can go both ways. Conflict should not be regarded as a purely negative issue. Conflict has a duel capacity. It can certainly tear down and destroy. It can also reveal areas for growth and work, aiding progress and maturity.

The conciliation principle

A powerful recognition of this tenet comes in the fifth chapter of Paul's letter to the Ephesians. Paul introduces his teaching on marriage with an insistence on conciliation in relationships. 'Submit to one another out of reverence for Christ' (5:21). Having established the overall principle that conciliatory attitudes provide a prime dynamic for strengthening relationships, Paul then goes on to spell out how in each case male and female partners are to work this out in practice.

'Wives, submit to your husbands as to the Lord' (5:22). 'Husbands, love your wives, just as Christ loved the church and gave himself up for her' (5:25). To submit means to yield your rights. That is exactly what Jesus did by becoming man, travelling the road which led eventually to the cross. He did not cling to his rights (Phil. 2:6).

In Paul's concept of the marriage relationship the injunction to man and woman are the same. Neither must cling to their rights. The husband's love must be characterised by loving sacrifice and servanthood. So indeed should the woman for she is to submit to her husband as she would to the Lord himself. Conciliation is a key concept in the maintenance of marriage equilibrium.

Two people pulling in opposite directions have a tug-of-war. They either end up in stalemate, or one of them gets dragged over the line. They cannot both succeed in attaining their mutually exclusive goals. By contrast, when Paul envisages a relationship of conciliation in marriage, a working together for common goals, the practical outworking involves both partners in constantly adjusting to the needs of the other.

The marriage vows of the Church of England reflect this principle. Each takes the other, 'To have and to hold, from this day forward, for better, for worse, for richer, for poorer, in sickness and in health, to love and to cherish, till death us do part' *(The Alternative Service Book*, CUP,

1980). The declaration of intent which precedes these vows implies a similar level of commitment and flexibility. It calls on each partner in turn to love, comfort, honour and protect; and forsaking all others, to remain faithful as long as both shall live.

All the historic churches have fashioned marriage vows which echo the teaching principles of Paul. His practicality which has been so readily distilled into such words is drawn from a theology which he describes as 'a profound mystery' (Eph. 5:32). The mystery is a quotation from the creation narrative, 'For this reason a man will leave his father and mother and be united to his wife, and the two will become one flesh' (Eph. 5:31 quoting Gen. 2:24).

Leaving and cleaving

The one-flesh relationship provides a practical unified view of marriage where man and woman are seen as deeply complementary to each other. This is a relationship closer even than that of child to parent. Children eventually become independent of their parents, whereas husband and wife belong together 'till death us do part'. The leaving and cleaving principle implies a progress into an exclusive, mature and enduring relationship whose closeness and bonding exceeds all others.

Man and woman are not, however, incomplete without each other, for that would devalue singleness, of which Jesus himself was a prime exemplar. But in marriage a kind of new creation takes place. The one-flesh nature of the relationship does not just refer to the sexuality of marriage; although sexuality in marriage is both an expression and symbol of that oneness. The one-flesh relationship refers to an enhanced humanness, which is the ideal of marriage. That is why Paul likens marriage to the relationship between Christ and his Church. Significantly, the Biblical picture of the Church perfected in heaven is of the outward beauty of a bride adorned for her husband, a beauty symbolising all that is pure and wholesome (cf. Rev. 21). That beauty is not just the goal for the Church; it is *terminus ad quem* of marriage.

Making it work

It is all very well to talk in ideals, the question is how can this enhanced human experience be worked at and given the tenderness of feeling which such a closeness of relationship implies? What are the particular building blocks for a stable and happy marriage, which both overcomes and makes use of conflict constructively and positively for growth and fulfilment?

Foundations are important in many realms of life. Marriages need them as much as buildings. In his teaching, Jesus points out the importance of firm foundations for the stability of our lives. He who hears his words and obeys them 'is like a man building a house, who dug down deep and laid the foundation on rock' (Luke 6:48).

Marriage is designed by God to be a lifetime's commitment. No one should embark on it without the most careful consideration. But for all the desirability of the help that may be given in careful marriage preparation, the experience of marriage itself brings to life many personal challenges. The importance of good foundations is clearly seen when dealing with the growth process which must inevitably take place if marriages are to survive, let alone flourish.

The foundation of love

When a couple get engaged and married, you would hardly think that anything could come between them. The loving glances and the warmth of affection of a couple are touching to see. But romance is one thing, living together without discomfort is another. It is important that a relationship continues to be built on love as the marriage grows and progresses. Not everyone experiences it in a heady way, but the chemistry of love can be gloriously overwhelming. Apart from the obvious enjoyment of this extended honeymoon stage, it does mean that the actual hard work of the relationship can be delayed, for nothing the young lovers do could ever spoil the bliss – at least for a short while! But chemistry has to give way to physics. The actions of love are just as important as the feelings. How can the feelings (and responsibilities) of love be converted into action?

Love in action

From the example of Jesus in the gospels, we learn the particular importance of forgiveness and acceptance. When applied to marriage these two 'inward' actions provide an approach to the marriage relationship which is powerful and constructive when present, and undermining and destructive when absent.

Forgiveness

Jesus taught the priority of forgiveness. In the Lord's prayer, he teaches us to pray, 'Forgive us our debts as we also have forgiven our debtors' (Matt. 6:12). In the parable of the unmerciful servant which (not without reason) comes immediately before Jesus's teaching on divorce, Jesus strongly emphasises the responsibility to forgive from the heart (Matt. 18:35). Even if someone should sin against you seven times a day, Jesus says you should forgive those seven times (Luke 17:4). Seven is a Biblical number of completeness, here implying complete forgiveness. Yet should there be any misconceptions of Jesus's seriousness on this matter, when asked by Peter if he should forgive seven times (perhaps interpreting Jesus as putting a limit on forgiveness) Jesus replies, 'I tell you not seven times but seventy-seven times' (Matt. 18:22).

The call to forgiveness is a priority which needs constant attention, partly because in marriage the closer you get to each other the greater will be the likelihood of hurt. Hurt happens in all relationships. It is, therefore, only natural to experience some pain when two different people from different backgrounds, with a different make-up and personal history, get together. No one is immune.

A long-held piece of advice to couples is to keep short accounts, and to get the differences sorted out right away. The ways of doing this vary and it depends on your personal skills. Some prefer to have a regular time when they purposely sit down and talk about themselves, their feelings and their hurts. Others manage better in a more spontaneous fashion. Whatever the manner of approach the fact that attention is given in this area is the most important factor. The following stages need working through.

Acknowledging anger

If an issue arises where one or other marriage partner is saddened, hurt or affronted by the other, the most important initial agreement is to communicate this to the other partner as soon as it is acceptable to them both to do so. Grand confrontations in restaurants or at other people's dinner parties are thus excluded. The important factor is to ventilate the anger. Anger is like a red light at the traffic lights. It tells us to stop. Danger is ahead. Red lights are for our benefit. Anger in a relationship can be viewed positively.

It is the responsibility of the angered party to communicate successfully and reasonably why he or she has felt anger. It is a dual responsibility, for the one who has caused the anger needs to show his or her commitment to putting right the anger reaction in some way. Thus if both partners have a commitment to listening and responding swiftly when conflict strikes, the permission to express emotion will be a healthy safety valve for the relationship, and a vital part of its ongoing maintenance.

Controlling anger

The next stage in this strategy for expressing the strains which give rise to hurt and resentment concerns a mutual agreement not to hurt, attack or retaliate. Slanging matches rarely achieve anything positive, and other anger responses can be even more destructive. Clearly there needs to be some measure of self-control in these situations, but it is easier if there has been a clear and prior agreement that disputes will be handled in this way. This in turn frees a couple to listen sensitively to each other.

We all have different learned responses to anger. Those who tend to retaliate need to work on ways of coping with the way their immediate strong feelings cause them to behave. If you do get heated, agree with each other to stand or sit far enough apart not to be able to push or shove. If you tend to throw things, put objects away or go out into the garden. You should, of course, learn to modify your responses, but realism demands you do something practical like this if you are a physically demonstrative person. This aspect of the strategy is just as purposeful and beneficial in the management of conflict as the agreement not to say hurtful and aggressive things. If you tend to express your anger with your actions, by seeing your committed efforts to modify your responses, your partner will be that much more encouraged to speak openly with the belief that he or she will receive a real and fair hearing.

Resolving anger

When the matter under discussion has been aired, the final element in this strategy is to agree to work the issue through together. It does not matter who is aggrieved, the issue belongs to both parties, and the owning, sharing and resolution of the matter brings great strength and sense of purpose to both parties.

In a close relationship, the anger of one is a function of both. Paul's principle of conciliation comes into play at this point. Like a pressure cooker in danger of becoming overheated, once the steam is released all is safe and well, and the cooking process can continue. When the steam is taken out of a tense marriage using this process of ventilation, work can continue on resolving the differences and building the quality and richness of the marriage. In fact, the conflict itself, properly handled in this way, should contribute positively to the relationship, for each partner will be closer to the other with greater mutual understanding and adjustment than before.

Creative tensions

Marriage tension is inevitable, but this kind of tension can, and should, be creative. Marriage conflicts are opportunities for growth. The creative way of handling tensions is to be prepared to forgive right from the beginning. This pledge of forgiveness lends great strength to marriage. It enables couples to grow and creatively overcome those painful moments which are part of every marriage. Forgiveness helps you steer round the obstacles, to grow more together. You don't run up a backlog of mutual resentment when forgiveness is present.

- Keep short accounts
- Keep talking

- Keep listening – to feelings as much as words
- Keep on forgiving
- When you forgive – forget

There you go again

There is a special danger in marriage conflicts. The catalogue of unforgiven wrongs simply grows and grows, as we saw in Barry and Helen's case. When we forgive, we have a model of forgiveness in Jesus. Our sins are completely dealt with. They are never brought up again to taunt or accuse us. Forgiveness is one of the most important parts of the marriage foundation. We can and should learn from this model. The Lord's Prayer teaches us that we should forgive in the same measure we have been forgiven. It also teaches us to realise how much we ourselves require God's forgiveness, and cannot claim self-righteousness. All this means the letting go of someone else's past. It means a commitment not to keep on bringing up, either in your mind or in conversation, the painful hurts of the past. Let them go. That is what forgiveness is about. It means never hearing yourself say, 'There he goes again'; 'There she goes again'.

Loving acceptance

All this implies a very deep acceptance of each other. This acceptance is the psychological dimension of the unity of the one-flesh relationship. Some people try to force their partner to be the person they want them to be. Yet in its essence love means acceptance. Love implies the acceptance of each other as you really are.

Acceptance enables you not to have to hide things about yourself and to find freedom to be yourself. When there is the experience of acceptance like this within a marriage, when you know you are truly loved and accepted, then there is the possibility of change and growth. Many couples enter into marriages with the highest intentions, and while the chemistry is most potent the intentions are more easily converted into action. The important decision is never to give up working for each other's benefit. We all need to work at forgiveness and acceptance right into our dotage.

The foundation of commitment

Love is a depends-what-you-mean word. It is all very well to talk about love, but it depends what you mean by it, for love is one of the most devalued terms and concepts in our language. Towards the end of his first letter to the Corinthians, Paul challenges the Corinthian Christians on the quality of their love, and in doing so has provided us with a bench-mark of quality as far as the practice of love is concerned. The famous words of 1 Corinthians 13 are all about commitment. Paul speaks of love in terms of behaviour, in fact as a commitment to behave in a certain kind of way. Paul shows how love can be practised.

'Love is patient, and kind; love is not jealous or boastful; it is not arrogant or rude. Love does not insist on its own way; it is not irritable or resentful; it does not rejoice at wrong, but rejoices in the right. Love bears all things, believes all things, hopes all things, endures all things' (1 Cor. 13:4–7 RSV).

If that sounds like a counsel of perfection, it is not meant to be, for Paul is showing the practicalities of love when put into action. This foundation of commitment means a decision to behave according to certain standards of conduct towards another person. These standards of conduct can be applied to marriage, for they are central to Paul's ethical understanding of the outworking of love.

Paul begins his 'definition' of love with the examples of patience and kindness. These both imply the importance of listening, not only to what the other says in words, but also to what the other feels. Some of us are not good at listening to feelings. Feelings sometimes are ignored. They are not always heard. Learning to listen to feelings is essential in any area of experience. It is a learning process. Especially in building a marriage of two different people with two different ways of looking at life.

Felt needs

We all have deeply felt needs beneath the surface. And we need kindness to respond to those deeply felt needs. Marriage makes us vulnerable. So time is needed for good listening, and the formation and expression of kindness and love. As marriages develop, couples can find themselves busier and busier. It is a fatal mistake to skimp on time for each other. For marriage is a commitment to maximise the happiness and the fulfilment of the one by the other. Patience, kindness, learning to listen to feelings as much as words: all such are needed in the foundation of commitment.

- 'Love is patient and kind'. What can you and your partner do to put this into practice towards each other at the moment?
- 'Love is not jealous or boastful'. Are there ways in which you should adjust your attitudes to your partner?
- 'Love is not arrogant or rude'. How, practically, can you apply this principle to your marriage relationship, especially when there is conflict?
- 'Love does not insist on its own way'. Can you find some practical ways of conciliation which will benefit your relationship at present?

- 'Love is not irritable or resentful'. Have you let a catalogue of hurts and wrongs build up? What are you going to do about it?
- 'Love does not rejoice at wrong, but rejoices in the right'. Are you aiming to bring encouragement and esteem to your partner? In what practical ways can you do this?
- 'Love bears all things, believes all things, hopes all things, endures all things'. When you are under pressure, do you really trust that God will uphold you? Will you decide now to make every effort to improve your marriage, however difficult?

The foundation in God

All couples face hurdles. As the divorce statistics imply, most couples face their fair share of hurdles in the first two years of marriage. But facing up to conflicts and difficulties throughout marriage, be it in the early years or later, is the way of growth and strength. According to Jesus, it is not possible to consider real foundations in marriage and in life without also considering the spiritual dimension to our lives. This involves more than just values, but where you are going, your direction, your knowledge and understanding of God's purposes for you personally. This may be why it is said that couples who pray together, stay together. It is not as simple as it sounds, but a shared openness to God in life and in marriage makes every difference. It is not so much a matter of praying together (good though that is), but of being one in purpose and spirit.

It is possible, however, to start off with good intentions, but to slip back on all these important elements once the pressure of circumstances begins to dictate. Yet Jesus is insistent. No building can stand without firm foundations, and neither can a marriage. The person who hears his words and obeys them 'is like a man building a house, who dug deep, and laid the foundation upon rock; and when a flood arose, the stream broke against that house, and could not shake it, because it had been well built' (Luke 6:48 RSV).

- What can you do to start rebuilding the foundations of your marriage?
- Ask each other what *one* manageable action you can perform which will bring the other happiness. Try doing it!
- Do you know what pleases your partner most? Try finding out. But don't be hoodwinked into thinking that gifts and other offerings are the way to bring *lasting* happiness. Gestures help. But it is the way you treat each other which matters most.
- Try asking, 'What can we do together that you would like to do?' You both need to do this to work at the principle of conciliation.
- Work on ventilating long-term resentments or hurts by asking, 'In what area would you like to see me change and why?' Keep to the rules of the three-stage strategy for resolving anger and conflict outlined earlier. Keep cool. Work it through. Do it together.

Breaking the bonds

As we saw earlier, attitudes to marriage are changing fast. An American handbook called *Divorce – how and when to let go* confidently affirms the easy destructibility of the marriage bond. 'Yes, your marriage can wear out. People want to experience new things. Change is part of life. Letting go of your marriage, if it is no longer good for you, can be the most successful thing you've ever done. Getting a divorce can be a positive, problem-solving, growth-orientated step. It can be a personal triumph.'

We are in a rapidly changing world as far as marriage and divorce are concerned. Between the years 1715 to 1852 the average number of divorces was less than two per year. When the psychiatrist Jack Dominian wrote his influential book on marital breakdown in 1968, that figure had soared to some 30,000 divorces every year. In 1986 in the United Kingdom, there was one marriage every 80 seconds, and a divorce once every 175 seconds! From 1989, with around 165,000 divorces per annum, we are getting on for almost one in two marriages ending in divorce.

Marriage crisis

We live in a world where there is an enormous pressure on the stability of marriage. Clearly there is much unhappiness. It is not putting it too strongly to say that marriage is in crisis not only in the UK, but throughout the Western world. Most of us know someone who is unhappy about their marriage situation. We are either in the situation ourselves or we are likely to know someone who is. It is therefore important to look at the Biblical teaching on the painful question of divorce. Too many too easily turn to divorce to solve their difficulties of conflict. But for some, however much we wish it to be otherwise, grounds for divorce seem pressing in the desperate unhappiness and pain either or both partners appear to be experiencing.

Jesus and divorce

'Some Pharisees came to him to test him. They asked, "Is it lawful for a man to divorce his wife for any and every reason?"'(Matt. 19:3).

The arguments were raging even then about marriage and divorce, and the matter was put to Jesus in a situation of controversy, for the Pharisees were playing politics, trying to get Jesus to take sides in the debate. Two schools of thought, led by influential rabbinic teachers, Shammai and Hillel, disagreed vehemently on their interpretations of a key Old Testament passage dealing with divorce. The issue concerned the opening statement: 'If a man marries a woman who becomes displeasing to him because he finds something indecent about her . . . ' (Deut. 24:1).

The conservative, Shammai, argued that 'indecent' referred to adultery, which alone was grounds for divorce. The liberal, Hillel, focused on the words 'a woman who becomes displeasing to him'. He concentrated on the woman becoming displeasing in general, not in the particular sense of adultery. Hillel advocated a whole range of displeasing behaviour as grounds for divorce, including spoiling the dinner; speaking to other men in the street; wearing unbound hair; speaking disrespectfully to the husband's parents in his presence; even if the wife's voice was so loud it could be overheard by the neighbours! Hillel's followers made the situation even worse. Later Rabbi Akabar ruled that 'a woman who becomes displeasing' meant a man could divorce his wife if he simply found a woman he liked better and considered more beautiful.

Jesus and first principles

'Haven't you read,' Jesus replied, 'that at the beginning the Creator made them male and female, and said, "For this reason a man will leave his father and mother and be united to his wife, and the two will become one flesh"? So they are no longer two but one. Therefore what God has joined together, let man not separate' (Matt. 19:4–6).

Jesus insists on clarity concerning the *nature* of marriage. It is not enough to say, 'Divorce if your marriage doesn't suit you,' for marriage is a one-flesh relationship. And Jesus adds his own comment on the Genesis passage from which the one-flesh teaching is taken, 'What God has joined together, let man not separate' (Matt. 19:6).

Jesus emphasises that marriage is a unique work of God. It is not simply a contractual relationship which can be ended at will, for what God has joined together cannot be ended lightly. Although a contract or covenant is involved, *marriage is a state of being, not just of belonging*. That thought is contained in the word 'wedding' which refers to this Biblical idea of being indissolubly 'wedded' to each other. Marriage is intended as a bond for life, and Jesus's appeal to first principles provides us with a high view of marriage, a vivid contrast to liberal teaching then and now.

Jesus and the human situation

'Jesus replied, "Moses permitted you to divorce your wives because your hearts were hard. But it was not this way from the beginning. I tell you that anyone who divorces his wife, except for marital unfaithfulness, and marries another woman commits adultery "' (Matt. 19:8).

The Pharisees had asked why Moses commanded that a man give his wife a certificate of divorce. (Matthew 19:7.) Jesus's reply displays great concern for what Moses actually said: 'Moses permitted you . . . ' (Not 'commanded you'.) The difference is of immense importance. The certificate of divorce was a simple but eventually abused means of effecting the divorce procedure. The woman had no rights in the matter, for by Jesus's time all the man had to do was to write out the words 'I divorce you' and the divorce was effected. Jesus points out that Moses did not *command* this. Moses *permitted* divorce because of the human realities involved, for it was meant to be a protection for the woman against the possibility of physically aggressive acts from the husband. There is no sense in which Moses commanded divorce. As Jesus says, it was permitted because of the hardness of men's hearts. Human realities are recognised, but in Jesus's teaching the lifelong marriage deal is nonetheless firmly upheld.

Jesus and the grounds of divorce

Remember Jesus was asked about the legality of divorce. His reply was authoritative, clarifying, and decisive. Jesus is clearly telling the Pharisees that a libertarian attitude to divorce is not acceptable. We do not have the freedom to do just what we like. Because marriage is a state of being, not just a contract, and it is ordained by God himself. Marriages cannot be ended at will or whim.

Jesus is also recognising the realities of human experience. It is possible so to violate the state of marriage, specifically by adultery, that in those circumstances divorce is conceivable and permissible. Thus Jesus is not countering the Pharisees' arguments with a new legalism of his own. Jesus's words, like Moses, are a concession and not a directive. Jesus understands the hardness of the human heart, and has compassion on those in marriage relationships who find their lives in turmoil and pain.

Paul's view

Our examination of the Biblical material needs also to listen to the teaching of Apostle Paul. Paul speaks of the pastoral situation of a Christian man or woman being married to someone who is not a Christian. Such a situation would have been very common then, and is increasingly common now. Paul's counsel to those in such a situation is that they should not divorce if the other partner is willing to stay. But note Paul's qualifying words, 'If the unbeliever leaves, let him do so. A believing man or woman in such circumstances is not bound' (1 Cor. 7:15).

Here then we have another concession. Notice that Paul does not tie himself legalistically to the details of Jesus's words. He would certainly have known the Lord's teaching on this important matter. But he doesn't say, 'Jesus says there is only one ground for divorce, and that is adultery.' By implication, he goes to the *heart* of what Jesus has been teaching. Sadly, a marriage of two people can be violated at the deepest level of trust and union. This must be Paul's reasoning as he applies Jesus's principle to another area of experience. If this were not so, Paul's words would have contradicted what Jesus teaches. Paul is applying a principle rather than a precept.

The background to Paul's conclusion is not complicated. Paul counsels that believers should not knowingly be married to those who are not followers of Christ. But where that is the case, however the marriage has been contracted, divorce and remarriage are both possible, if divorce appears the only option. That will only be so if the unbelieving partner is to leave, because at that point the values and foundations of the marriage are shown to be violated and at odds.

So taking the overall position of Scripture on this matter, it is clear there is no Biblical set of rules and regulations for divorce and remarriage as such. What we do have, however, is one supreme foundation principle. Marriage is designed and intended to be a lifelong one-flesh relationship. Moses, Jesus and Paul all recognise the human realities involved. Marriages can fail, and divorce is sometimes necessary. But in spite of what is often claimed, there is no such thing as a dead marriage. There can be failure, hurt, violation and muddle. Some marriages can appear practically lifeless with little hope. Yet change is possible where there is willingness that progress should take place.

Marriage under pressure

If you are one of the unfortunate ones facing misery in your marriage, let me say with sensitivity and understanding that God does and will sustain those in deeply unhappy relationships, especially those in marriages where one partner simply refuses to do anything to help the situation. All our efforts and prayers should be directed towards getting both partners to co-operate in finding help. Marital pathology is fully recognised by those who give support through marriage counselling. It means that we bring our disordered lives right into marriage more than we do in any other kind of relationship. That is why the assistance of a trained, skilled and sympathetic third party is of such help when marriage conflict gets out of hand.

Selfishness is one of the biggest problems in marriages. 'If each partner comes to regard marriage as primarily a quest for his or her self-fulfilment, rather than as an adventure in reciprocal self-giving, through which parents and children grow into maturity, then the outlook is likely to be bleak' (John Stott, *Issues Facing Christians Today*, Marshalls, 1984). It is really worth saying to all who are married or who will be one day, and particularly to those who are maintaining painful relationships, you must work at being generous to your partner. That means giving yourself, and giving yourself, and giving yourself, over and over again. You have to pick yourself up when you get rebuffed for the thousandth time, and despite the discouragement, don't lose heart. After all, if you have hurt each other, your husband or wife may take quite some convincing that you truly mean it when you say you are really going to change. But give yourself you must, for selfishness must be conquered.

Taking stock

All this takes time and a great deal of patience and application. It means taking stock of what is important in your life. It means taking practical decisions about the use of time. Those who put their work or other considerations before their family life often live to regret it. It means soul-searching and prayer. It means not going it alone. It requires the love and support of close family and friends.

What are proper grounds for divorce? As the law stands in England and Wales there is only one ground, namely that the marriage has irretrievably broken down. In order to demonstrate this breakdown, proof is required for one or more of these five facts:

- That the respondent has committed adultery and the petitioner finds it intolerable to live with the respondent.
- That the respondent has behaved in such a way that the petitioner cannot reasonably be expected to live with the respondent.
- That the respondent has deserted the petitioner for a continuous period of at least two years immediately preceding the presentation of the petition.
- That the parties have lived apart for a continuous period of at least two years immediately preceding the presentation of the petition and that the respondent agrees to a decree being granted.
- That the parties have lived apart for at least five years immediately preceding the presentation of the petition.

A petition for divorce cannot be presented until one year has elapsed since the marriage was formalised, whatever the circumstances may be. Judicial separation proceedings can be started at any time should the full protection of court proceedings be required.

These are the pure legalities of divorce proceedings. But what is the case from a Biblical and Christian perspective? Some would say that only two 'facts' exist: adultery, and the desertion of an unbelieving partner. Others will say there are further matters which can destroy the very heart of a marriage and lead to irretrievable breakdown. Both Jesus and Paul will say that marriage is designed to be a one-flesh lifelong relationship, but they both recognise the human realities. It is only when everything else has genuinely been tried that divorce can ever be contemplated. Jesus's words are intended to put a stop to liberal divorce practices, and an all-too-easy acceptance of failure when more can be done.

Facing facts

If you have been through a divorce, you must have asked yourself, what if I'd handled things differently? How would things be today? The answer is you cannot change the past. God takes us as we are. The Lord who says, 'I hate divorce' (Mal. 2:16) also affirms 'I will heal their waywardness and love them freely, for my anger has turned away from them' (Hos. 14:4). We believe in a God who offers complete forgiveness where there has been failure, and new strength for the future day by day.

We all have a responsibility to help those who are married, as well as upholding with sympathetic love those whose marriages have failed. The pressures today from our society are enormous. Housing, money, unemployment, family and in-laws, religion, sexual expectations and sexual difficulties. All these add to the pressure. Above all the drift to a self-seeking, self-satisfying, self-fulfilling approach to relationships is where the rot is really setting in.

If you are facing the facts in your relationship or that of someone close to you, be encouraged. There is forgiveness and a new start for all those who follow Christ. There is a power and strength available from the Holy Spirit which means it is truly possible to change in reliance on him. We should look with deep understanding and compassion upon those whose relationships have failed or are in danger of failing. But let's also resolve to do something to help. Prayer makes such a difference. And there may be something you should be doing to help your own situation or the situation of someone else. As a Christian, as you observe the lives of others, perhaps you are in a situation of stability. Do give thanks, but remember this; it is always a case of there but for the grace of God go I.

MARRIAGE RELATIONSHIPS

- Review the lessons you have learned in this chapter.
- What are the most important insights you have gained?
- Work out a personal timetable for putting these thoughts into practice.
- What can you do to help yourself and your partner?
- What can you do to help someone else?
- Work through the marriage vows. Think about their implications for you and for your partner. Then work at them together. You may want (and need) to choose a suitable time to reaffirm these vows again to each other. 'I (your name) take you (your partner's name) to be my wife (husband), to have and to hold, from this day forward, for better, for worse, for richer, for poorer, in sickness and in health, to love and to cherish, till death us do part, according to God's holy law; and this is my solemn vow.'
- Spend some moments working out on paper the most important issues you need to pray about.
- Now meditate on these words of Paul, thinking about what they tell you about the grace and love of God in your own situation or that of someone close to you. Use this knowledge of God's care as you spend some moments praying through the issues you have isolated in the points above.

'Praise be to the God and Father of our Lord Jesus Christ, the Father of compassion and the God of all comfort, who comforts us in all our troubles, so that we can comfort those in any trouble with the comfort we have received from God' (2 Cor. 1:3–4).

Part Three

Inner Conflict

7

CONFLICTS OF SPIRIT

Conflict affects us in a variety of ways. Conflict doesn't just involve us in disputations with others. Conflict often takes place within ourselves. It is felt as a tussle of will, a powerful urge to transgress standards of thought or behaviour which only a part of us declares as inviolable. It is something akin to a child's musing choice to disobey a parent, 'Shall I or shan't I?' Inner conflict involves the experience of temptation, the seduction of ambition and often a struggle with God, perceived or unrealised.

Our inner world

Inner conflict has as much potential for good as it does evil, for the conflicts experienced provide opportunities for mature choices, as well as self-luxuriating indulgences. Conflict and the potential for growth therefore belong together. In this chapter, we'll be looking at the conflicts of our inner world in relation to God's purposes for the development of our wholeness and maturity. The struggle for freedom of mind and spirit is always linked in the Bible with the embrace of God's will for our lives. That it is a struggle is evidenced both by the substance of God's commandments to his people, and by the experience of those who are held up to us as examples of the kind of living faith which overcomes the pressing difficulties of inner conflict of these kinds.

Wouldn't it be lovely . . .

Imagine yourself in your favourite shopping street. It's a lovely sunny afternoon. You have money in your pocket, a cheque-book on you and one or two credit cards as well. It is a strange sensation, but many sense it from time to time: a consuming desire to part with money. That reckless spending feeling has gripped you.

On your walkabout, you notice that your favourite department store have their sale on. It's their thirty-second sale of the year. How do they do it? But just look at that suite of furniture. Only £5,000. Save £4,999. It has to be a bargain!

Your heart starts beating faster. Your mind begins to race. But just feel that adrenalin as you walk farther along the road. Look at that latest low-light video camera in the photo store; the striped green leather moccasins in that new rather up-market shoe shop; the new designer range of clothes next door. To say nothing of the cut-price Caribbean cruise, the satellite-TV dish and the fully computerised Cosworth car at a cool £25,000 from the newly opened Ford dealers. As you come to the end of your Saturday afternoon stroll, your mind is full of enticing possibilities.

Enjoy now, pay later

Wouldn't it be lovely to be rich? Maybe it would. But the dread disease of covetousness afflicts even the very wealthy. A strange fact about those of us who live in the West is that we always seem to want more than we have. Such an attitude provides the inner experience of conflict for many. It is enthusiastically fuelled by the advertisers and made respectable by successive governments of all countries who make consumerism into a *summum bonum*. Yet covetousness goes farther than material things alone. It touches some very deep questions as to what we are as people, and how we react to a variety of inner desires and temptations. It's not just the excitement of going shopping and using your plastic flexible friends to enjoy now and pay later.

You shall not covet

The tenth commandment raises this issue in a most searching and relevant way. 'You shall not covet your neighbour's house. You shall not covet your neighbour's wife, or his manservant or maidservant, his ox or donkey, or anything that belongs to your neighbour' (Exod. 20:17).

Since these words are of such great antiquity, recorded some three and a half thousand years ago, how are they still relevant today, especially in relation to the inner conflicts of our lives? To discover the impressive contemporary relevance of such imperatives, we need to establish what we mean when we speak of covetousness, and what is envisaged in the Bible by the idea of coveting.

Entertainment value

Many of the TV soap operas exploit covetousness. *Dynasty* is one of many and has enjoyed some huge ratings. In one episode, the usual cliffhanger excitement was almost literal at the end as Alexis and Dex went hurtling over the balcony. But whatever had happened to unsettle their dignity, they had spent the whole episode in usual fashion (along with Blake, Jeff, Adam, Sammy Jo, Fallon, Monica and Sable and the rest) all scheming away, trying to get each other's money, destroying each other's reputation and jumping into bed with those they had no right to. It is all done very cheerfully, and you can hardly believe in the characters as real people, though these personality weaknesses are very real and recognisable.

It is noticeable how *Dynasty*, *Dallas*, and many other soaps on TV tend to focus on this kind of human weakness, often exploiting covetousness. The impulse to covetousness provides much of the subject matter for the human battles of their story lines. Plastic and unbelievable though the characters may be, yet realistic and true to life are the human temptations and struggles involved.

The power to destroy

What happens when the coveting feeling takes a hold? When people covet it makes them greedy. Covetousness can cause stealing. Such greed can drive people to sacrifice the well-being of others. It can lead to murder in extreme cases. Covetousness affects relationships. It gives rise to lust. The kind of lust which can end up in adultery, extramarital sex, or unsought pregnancies. It can lie behind much human unhappiness, including dissatisfaction, depression and divorce.

Covetousness is comprehensive. It can be directed towards objects, money or sex, as well as inner feelings. It can lead people to lie about themselves, destroying trust and love. It can be an attempt to gain wealth, power, prestige or praise. Above all, covetousness has enormous power and potential to destroy. To destroy us *and* others.

Old sayings

There is a logic to the ancient tenth commandment, 'You shall not covet your neighbour's house ... wife, or his manservant or maidservant, his ox or donkey, or anything that belongs to your neighbour' (Exod. 20:17). It is because God loves us and desires the best for our humanness and growth that he declares a law against covetousness. The enticement to covet is like the attraction of an enchanting perfume, one which turns out to be a delicious, attractive, sweet-tasting poison. It is highly beguiling, but it has power to stifle and to kill.

Every nation and culture has sayings and proverbs about covetousness. It is often said, 'The grass is always

CONFLICTS OF SPIRIT

greener on the other side of the fence.' There is a Scottish proverb which puts its point delightfully: 'The covetous man will *never* have enough – until his mouth is filled with mould.' A Hindu proverb is just as vivid: 'If you mention money, even the corpse opens wide its mouth.'

There is a widespread recognition of the reality of covetousness. Yet despite that recognition, only in the Bible do you find the true nature, extent and solution to covetousness clearly spelt out. The Bible recognises covetousness; it also has a solution to it. And no other culture, no other religion in the world, goes so deep.

The nature of covetousness

Though much of the Bible deals with the outworking of the dangers of coveting in practice, the tenth commandment is the place where the matter is dealt with starkly and specifically, and with deeper insight into its inner workings. All the other commandments involve specific actions. Don't do this. Do that. But the tenth commandment is different from all the rest. The tenth commandment is not about an action, it's about an attitude. It's inward rather than external. It forbids an attitude rather than an action.

This teaches that covetousness is a state of mind and heart. It introduces into the Bible the idea that wrong thoughts and wrong desires *precede* wrong actions. That lays a foundation for the teaching of Jesus many years later, 'For out of the heart come evil thoughts, murder, adultery, sexual immorality, theft, false testimony, slander' (Matt. 15:20). The principle we can distil from this is that thoughts precede actions.

- Can you think of times when the desire to covet has gripped your thoughts?
- What specific areas were you coveting, and why do you interpret this as coveting as such?

- How did the thoughts take hold of you?
- What did you do to let the thoughts remain or to rid yourself of them?

There are fifty-nine references in the teaching of Jesus to the importance of the heart in this respect. His teaching is clear that wrong desires precede wrong actions. In working through the whole question of the handling of desire, the commandment deals with the power of the attitude itself and not just the power of deeds which provide the allurement and attraction.

Out of control

Anthea had an obsessional spending problem. She had been thrown into a crisis because the credit card companies had caught up with her and demanded payment. But Anthea's real problem was not really with her spending at all. Underneath the spending problem was a bad mental habit. She had taught herself to indulge her desires. The idea of wanting things really came to rule over her. There was a passion, an enormous inner appetite to buy and possess things, and a desire for instant gratification. Whatever the cause, and it had something to do with her thwarted desire for self-assertion and power, it was nevertheless a bad case of covetousness. It is one thing to understand the pressures on us to behave in certain ways. But in Anthea's case, she was capable of behaving otherwise. She needed the discipline which the law of God provides to tame the worse excesses of her covetousness.

In the same way as some read pornography to feed their sexual desires, Anthea would spend ages reading adverts. She consumed all the advertisements and catalogues she could get her hands on. She became obsessed with buying things. Always wanting more than it was ever right, wise

CONFLICTS OF SPIRIT 159

or practical for her to have. She fed her desire daily. Happily, Anthea is fine now. She *used* to say, again and again, 'I can't control my spending. I can't stop myself. I can't do anything about it.' But when she saw the problem was not the spending itself, but the attitude at work behind the spending, then there was progress. When she worked on her inner attitudes, then the change came.

Anthea's situation raises the question, what is going on underneath the surface? It is a question all of us must raise about ourselves if we are to understand the pressures and conflicts of our inner world.

Instant gratification

The desire for instant gratification builds a guzzling pressure inside. In a sense, a young child is a prisoner of desire. A child will scream till he gets what he wants. This goes back to early feeding and toilet practices. But as soon as the child begins to grow, instant requirements give way to patience. The biscuit tin is safe on the table. Others can enjoy their meal in relative peace, since needs are learning to wait their turn.

Delayed gratification is a sign of growing maturity, a way that adults properly respond to the world. The desire for instant gratification can represent immaturity and arrested development in this aspect of the personality. Once recognised in an adult, it can be tamed and re-educated, just as a child will be patiently shown ways of coping with delay by its loving parents.

Life on the inside

'Greed ... is idolatry' (Col. 3:5). Paul's words give us some kind of clue to this inner attitude. We should be clear from the outset that desire in itself is not wrong.

For a school-leaver who has worked hard at exams, the desire to go off to college or university or get a good job is not wrong. For an actor who has worked hard at a role, the desire for good notices is not wrong. For a cook who has spent the entire day in the kitchen, the desire that the dinner guests should have a wonderful evening is not wrong.

Desire is not wrong when it is motivated towards a good end. Desire for material things is not necessarily wrong either, since material things in themselves are good. We have simply to *tame* our desires so that, for instance, our spending is responsible.

Wanting things

Desire for material things is not necessarily wrong at all, though many get worried at the thought of being labelled materialistic. Christians can get a distorted picture when it comes to possessions. Theologically we need to be clear on the truth that God is Creator. Our Creator has made a beautiful, material world, and that material world is meant to be richly enjoyed. At creation God declared that it was good. We know the world is fallen, but it is still *good* in essence, not evil.

Certain responses follow. The truth of God as Creator means we should be life-affirming, not life-denying. Asceticism is the philosophy which denies the value of material things. You give up everything. You may take a vow of poverty, chastity and obedience, and there are indeed many sincere people who take this line. But from a Christian position, in spite of the centuries of monastic tradition, can this be defended Biblically?

The evil of desire?

The Bible does not teach asceticism. We are not meant to be self-indulgent and we are meant to take responsibility for the poor – but we are not meant to be ascetic either.

CONFLICTS OF SPIRIT

Equally distorted on this point is the outlook of Buddhism. The Buddha taught that desire is the source of all evil in the world, and our life's pilgrimage must be to rid ourselves of desire of each and every sort.

In a way it sounds right. We have already established that desire can and does get out of hand. But not all desire is wrong. The idea that you *can* and *should* rid yourself of every kind of desire is in fact impractical and misconstrued. It denies our humanness. It denies our sexuality, our physical desires. It denies our creativity, our artistic desires. It denies our industry, our desire for purposeful use of time in work, leisure, sport and recreation. It's really *how* desire is handled that is crucial. And that's why God's commandments go so deep.

So when Paul says 'greed is idolatry', the key word is idolatry. Idolatry is putting someone or something in the place of God. It *is* possible for our own desires to take the place of God. Distorted desires are a grave defect. They take up so much inner energy. You find yourself thinking about something, day in, day out. It's a kind of lust, even if it is non-sexual and directed towards objects, activities or something else. The desire for instant gratification. I must have it. I must own it. It must be mine. We fix our gaze on something we do not have, so that we don't praise God for what we *do* have.

- What desires do you have which on reflection you consider wrong or unhelpful for you?
- Why do you consider them wrong?
- Do you feel the pressure for instant gratification?
- Is there anything in your upbringing or experience which accounts for this?
- In what areas do you feel it?
- What practical measure can you take to make progress on this?
- Spend some moments doing a time audit for the day. Try thinking back to what has filled your thoughts.

Are there any particular desires taking up this space and energy?
- What is it that you do not have that deflects your thankfulness to God for what you do have?

Covetousness is an inward attitude. As Jesus taught, it's attitudes which precede actions. This is why the attitudes need fixing first of all.

The extent of covetousness

We need to look at the areas where covetousness most powerfully enters our daily experience. Three major areas are touched on in the tenth commandment. (Exod. 20:17). They can be summarised as materialism, sex and money. For each of the items referred to is just one example of the comprehensive areas involved. 'Your neighbour's house' refers to belongings. 'Your neighbour's wife, manservant or maidservant' refers to relationships, particularly in this instance relationships which are out of bounds. The reference to the ox or donkey is to do with wealth and money, for in ancient Israel ownership of animals was an indication of your overall wealth. So covetousness touches on those desires which we all experience even today.

Health check

Is there an area of your life where covetousness is at work in relation to these major areas of materialism, sex and money? The way to work it out is this. You'll need to think about how energetically your inner desires are working on these issues.

Again, don't get this out of perspective. Don't confuse desire with covetousness. It's only when desire gets out of hand that you enter the danger zone. That's when desire becomes covetousness. As suggested above, you can get a clue to this if you monitor your 'thinking' time. How much time do you spend thinking about material things, sex or money? And it is not just a question of the time alone, but the inner energy and commitment you give daily to such thoughts.

Then contemplate the thoughts themselves. Are your thoughts pure? Or do you know they are thoughts of which God does not approve? Remember temptations are not wrong in themselves. It's what you do with temptation which matters.

Ambition

It is possible and very common also to covet position, esteem and power. When, for instance, does healthy ambition degenerate into covetousness?

In some circles ambition is a tainted word. It's gained itself a questionable reputation. Some of us are embarrassed to admit to it at all. It doesn't sound good. But admit to it or not, in many professions ambition is the very stuff of life.

If you are the kind of person who has dreams and aspirations, imagine yourself on one of those late-night chat shows. It is the probing personal interview. The chat show host puts his question. 'Are you ambitious?' he asks. You go slightly coy. You're probably more worried who will be watching and what they'll think. 'Well, not ambitious exactly. I do have certain goals. Things I'd like to achieve. New heights. Challenges. Yes, challenges. There are challenges ahead. Lots of challenges.'

You're lying through your teeth. Of course, you're ambitious. You've nursed your dreams for years. You are a driven person. It's better to admit it, at least to yourself; and ambition is one of the things that drive you.

There is something not quite nice about ambition. At least some think that. Look what it does to you. 'Vaulting ambition which o'erleaps itself.' It makes people climb and clamber over everybody else. It's the desire to reach the top of the pile, no matter who you tread on in the process. It's the insatiable drive to be rich, to be acclaimed, to be adored. It's that inner passion for recognition and praise, to be hailed as supreme, a master of your art or craft.

No wonder such a way is impossible for Christians. Is there an unspoken eleventh commandment: 'Thou shalt not be ambitious.' Doesn't ambition do violence to everything we stand for as Christians? Humility, patience, faith, dependence? Shouldn't we just admit it? Ambition is a sin. And we are all better off without it.

Or are we?

The truth is there is no eleventh commandment. Ambition is *not* wrong in itself. There would never be any achievements in the arts and sciences, and a host of other worthwhile and responsible activities, if men and women had not worked hard with commitment and energy to achieve their goals. But it is possible to covet position, esteem and power. It is possible to want the right thing for the wrong reasons. That is when ambition degenerates into covetousness.

- What are your ambitions?
- How pure are your motives?

Longings

A young minister said privately that he longs to become a famous Christian speaker. He wants to be a Billy Graham. But he admitted that his motives were mixed and that he was coveting the position of others. Someone else said he does everything he can to make others look up to him. He covets the esteem of others.

A twenty-four-year-old office worker spends a small fortune on clothes, with new outfits, dresses and shoes, every week. She says she longs to receive approval from others. She's consumed by her need. She uses her appearance to win that approval. She covets praise from others.

A fifty-year-old civil servant is unusually assertive and difficult in all kinds of meetings. He once admitted that for him power is like a drug. He will do everything he can to exert power over others. He has a lust for power. And it's all to do with covetousness. Covetousness is wide ranging. It touches all human activities.

Overcoming covetousness

The apostle Paul gives us some helpful clues to overcoming the inner conflict which covetousness produces. He wrote the following words from the Mamartine prison in Rome:

> I rejoice greatly in the Lord that at last you have renewed your concern for me. Indeed, you have been concerned, but you had no opportunity to show it. I am not saying this because I am in need, for I have learned to be content whatever the circumstances. I know what it is to be in need, and I know what it is to have plenty. I have learned the secret of being content in any and every situation, whether well fed or hungry, whether living in plenty or in want. I can do everything through him who gives me strength (Phil. 4:10–13).

It is important for us to realise the cramped conditions of his captivity, and the tiny cell deep beneath the ground from which he writes. We can appreciate the sense of reality behind his statements and the truthfulness with which he speaks.

Field of battle

Most of us find that there are times when we can describe our inner world as a battleground. We are all like this.

We have powerful inner cravings. Later we shall need to examine aspects of the battle which rages around the question of our spiritual allegiance. But for now we should notice what Paul says about the human ability to overcome covetousness. He calls it the secret of being content. And that secret is something that you *learn*.

Learn the secret

How do you learn the secret of being content? It is really a matter of co-operation between you and God. 'I can do everything through him who gives me strength' (Phil. 4:13). That's also a promise you can claim. 'Lord, help me overcome my weakness. Help me to break with my wrong attitudes and goals. Lord, I am going to drop this wrong aspiration. I am going to give it up. I am going to obey you.' And Jesus says when we obey him then he will give us strength and power. 'If you love me, you will obey what I command. And I will ask the Father and he will give you . . . the Spirit of truth' (John 14:15–16). The power flows from our obedience. We have to co-operate with God to show him that we are serious about following his will.

Shedding the dross

How do you get rid of a wrong attitude? A wrong attitude ends when you decide to let go of it, and no longer give it house room. In a way it's as simple as that. It's also preventive medicine, because when you let go of a wrong *attitude*, you prevent the occurrence of a wrong *action*. Most of us know where our weaknesses are. If we stop feeding our desires, they'll trouble us less and less.

We all need an inner spring-clean from time to time. The effort is certainly worth the trouble. When God says, 'You shall not covet' it is an indication of his will for us, that we should learn to deal with what goes on, not on the surface, but deep down inside.

CONFLICTS OF SPIRIT

- What wrong thoughts do you need to rid yourself of?
- Do you need to help yourself by disposing of magazines or books, or something else which feeds your wrong desires?
- Are there people you should decide to avoid?
- Are there places you should decide not to go?
- Do you want to glorify God in your inner attitudes?
- Spend a moment in prayer taking your stand on God's promise through Paul. 'I have learned the secret of being content in any and every situation ... I can do *everything* through him who gives me strength.'

Struggling with God

It is always possible to rationalise the conflicts within us. Most of our experiences are capable of explanation if only we were in full possession of all the details of our lives. Yet the fact that inner conflict can be explained in origin is not to say that we have dealt with the full weight of its significance. For these inner struggles we experience are often the battleground of other forces.

Principalities and powers

Paul is clear that 'our struggle is not against flesh and blood' alone, but against 'the powers of this dark world ... the spiritual forces of evil' (Eph. 6:12). We need not fear these powers, for as James comments, 'Resist the devil, and he will flee from you' (Jas. 4:7). Yet we should be warned, for the devil's scheme is to drag the believer away from God and deceive him about his true allegiance. This is why the full context of James's remark should be studied.

James speaks of the inner struggle we have been analysing as 'desires that battle within you' (Jas. 4:1). He speaks of coveting as asking with wrong motives 'that you may spend what you get on your pleasures' (Jas. 4:3).

He analyses the spirituality of this encounter with false values and motivations with devastating candour: 'Don't you know that friendship with the world is hatred towards God? Anyone who chooses to be a friend of the world becomes an enemy of God. Or do you think Scripture says without reason that the spirit he caused to live in us envies intensely' (Jas. 4:4–5).

James characterises the whole experience of this inner battle of the spirit by his quotation from the book of Proverbs, 'God opposes the proud but gives grace to the humble' (Jas. 4:6, quoting Prov. 3:34). This is the full background to James's thinking on the struggle experienced by the believer. 'Submit yourselves, then, to God. Resist the devil and he will flee from you. Come near to God and he will come near to you' (Jas. 4:7–8).

Submit to God

What does it mean to submit yourself to God? This inner tussle of will, these powerful urges to transgress God-given standards of thought or behaviour, the seductiveness of temptation or ambition, these are indeed a struggle with God, whether perceived or unrealised. The Bible links the struggle for freedom of mind and spirit with the embrace of God's will for our lives. If we are to find freedom, we have to find freedom in God. This is a powerfully taught principle throughout the Bible. It is highlighted particularly in the lives of the Patriarchs, Abraham, Isaac and Jacob. Jacob specifically is a man famed in the history of God's people as the one who struggled with God.

Jacob's story

Jacob was the son of Isaac and Rebekah. At first he appears as a most unpleasant character. He had an undistinguished beginning, cheating his brother, Esau, of his birthright, only gaining his father's blessing by impersonating his brother when his father had gone blind. He was a man of unruly temperament and powerful emotions. When Esau planned to kill him he escaped to Haran and had a dream of a staircase to heaven in which God spoke and promised him the land on which he slept. Later there came a strange wrestling match with an unknown 'man'. It was an experience of wrestling with God, from which Jacob ultimately received God's blessing.

In that strange encounter God and Jacob struggled together. Eventually this unruly man, Jacob, with all his faults, problems and open defiance of God and his ways, gave in. He let God be God. He let God take hold of his life. For ever after his descendants would be known not as sons of Jacob, but as sons of Israel. The very name, Israel, means to struggle with God. They too would struggle. God will prevail. Ultimately, as the Bible declares, he will use them for his purpose and glory.

Jacob today

In a sense, Jacob graduated. He eventually became the man that God could rely on, but only with many struggles. Seeing Jacob's life as a whole enables us to see someone with the same failings and inner conflicts as any of us today. He was a mass of contradictions, sensitivities and jealousy. Yet he was the one God used. His life, perhaps more than any other described in detail in the Bible, was a struggle with God. His new name, Israel, enshrines that for ever (see Gen. 35:9). But God used a man like that. In one sense God risked the future of his entire salvation plan on him.

Our struggles

God takes a risk with us, too. If your life has been touched by God in any way, and you find yourself struggling, there is an ultimate explanation for that. God brings evil on no one. But whatever the human explanations may be, our everyday lives contain all kinds of opportunities either to serve and honour God or to rebel and dishonour him. And once God has his hand upon you, he will be doing everything in his power to help you become what he knows you ought to be. 'God opposes the proud, but gives grace to the humble' (Prov. 3:34). But what God means as help may in the short term involve discomfort and soul-searching, as cherished hopes and ways become defeated or disarmed by circumstance.

- Do the lessons of Jacob's struggles shed light on any internal struggles you may be facing?
- What is God saying to you about the inner tensions that you face?
- Are your inward conflicts indicative of a mind in tune or out of phase with God's purposes?
- Will you aim to come into line with the Lord's will for you, and for your priorities?

No games

Jacob's story contains both an encouragement and a warning. The encouragement is clear: you are never too bad to be used by God. Jacob started life as a pretty nasty piece of work. We can see the evidence of God's power to change and transform a person. But the warning is equally distinct. Jacob struggled with God. The more we rebel the greater the struggle will be. Once God puts his hand on your life, he will not let you turn your back on him whatever you do, whether unwise, disobedient or openly sinful. Yet God will not give up on you. That means the struggle can sometimes be very hard, however young or old you happen to be.

CONFLICTS OF SPIRIT

This is the explanation behind many of the discomforts and wranglings of our inner conflicts. It involves obedience to a God who knows and loves us with a wisdom and passion way beyond human understanding. At its simplest, if you find yourself struggling, indeed wrestling with God, it is because he loves you. Like Jacob, he wants you to be a part of his people and his salvation plan. The fact is, you cannot play games with God. And Jacob's story proves it.

Part Four

Resolving Conflict

8

NEW WAYS TO RESPOND

All human interaction involves give and take within our communication processes. I may storm into a local store complaining loudly that the video I bought a year ago has broken down in the middle of my favourite TV programme. With a highly confrontational what-are-you-going-to-do-about-it attitude, I may berate the nearest salesperson. Depending on the tolerance level of the assistant concerned, I could in consequence endanger the possibility of constructive response. A more sober approach, with a quieter initial explanation avoiding recrimination, may be far more powerful in its effect.

Watchdogs

The disagreements between consumers and suppliers provide an extremely common example of interpersonal conflict. Part of the interest in consumer watchdog programmes on TV is not just the laudable aim of improving the quality of goods, services and consumer justice. The conflicts generated by such encounters boost the viewing figures in their own right. Will the best or mightiest man or woman win?

On both sides of the Atlantic, such consumer squabbles betray a hint of more overtly confrontational pastimes. Maybe as with wrestling or boxing this is an indication of the extent to which aggressive confrontationalism plays an important role in our human experience. In many areas, under the guise of entertainment, television provides a moderately harmless and diverting safety valve by which the pent-up steam of our everyday encounters can be partially and cathartically released.

Style and conflict

Difficulties in consumer affairs are much the same as in any other area of conflict. Where fraudulent, careless, or inconsiderate suppliers are involved, there may be a genuine grievance, and prevarication or procrastination will frustrate the matter further. Yet as recent surveys show, consumer complaints and grouses can as often be initiated by a misplaced grievance as by any legitimate charge.

When we come to consider the wide spectrum of interpersonal conflicts, many are made worse, and sometimes caused in themselves, by the attitudes and behaviour which clothe the communication process.

The verbal and body signals we give out, and the attitudes of mind which underlie them, may or may not reflect our intentions. But like a pianist playing a honky-tonk piano, if everything is out of tune, whatever the intention of the player, the music will sound distorted, dissonant and unpleasant to the ear. Conflicts in general are not necessarily tied to matters of fact or dispute. We can create conflicts simply by our manner, attitude, and verbal and listening styles.

One-sided conversation

A member of the family telephones after a long period of apparent neglect. There's a sharp response waiting and it's difficult to get a word in edgeways.

'It's Peter. I just phoned to . . .'
'I am sorry, which Peter?'
'Your brother, Peter. I thought I'd phone to . . .'

'I thought it was you. I suppose you have only phoned to ask me to do something for you. Well you listen to me, Peter, you only ever phone when you're in trouble or you need support. It would be nice if you had the time to enquire after any of us for a change. Just once, Peter. Just once. Frankly I'd rather not hear from you if it's always going to be so one-sided . . .'

Peter listened. He hardly said a word. Why does his brother never seem to hear what he says, let alone give him the chance even to complete a sentence? Peter got barked at again. Hardly a chance to get a word in. And he'd only phoned to wish his brother happy birthday . . .

Distortions

Poor and prejudicial listening is just one example of the way we can unintentionally distort the communication process, creating or contributing to conflict as a result. When conflict involves other people in this way, the way we react and respond is of vital importance. Often it is not possible to alter the nature of the conflict itself. A dispute with a local shop; a family member with fixed and determined views; a colleague with an inflexible, unsympathetic or biased attitude; all these are conflict factors which initially are fixed and unchangeable. If in the short term it may not look possible or hopeful to introduce any significant alteration or modification into the situation by way of discussion or other attempts at change, the *way* we respond can make some significant difference.

Fright and flight

When a cat encounters danger, its fur bristles, its back arches, purrs give way to hisses, and claws are poised to snatch and scratch. The eyes are widened in a freezing glance to take in the whole situation. The cat is transformed from soft-furred pet into screaming aggressor. It is ready for the fight in moments. It has learned no other way.

Human beings can react in the same manner. We, too, speak of putting our backs up. When we interpret a threat in some situation we can experience a similar fright and flight reaction. The muscle system is activated. The breathing rate increases. The mouth and throat may go dry. The voice trembles. Eyelids blink. Hands, knees and chest may tremble. But what happens *next* depends on how well we have learned to master or suppress anger, rage, fear and aggression.

We may share many characteristics with the instinctual behaviour of animals. But unlike the animal world we do not function on a purely instinctual basis alone. We have enormously powerful resources to modify our behaviour. Human beings can and should be in a constant mode of learning, aiming to modify thoughts, reactions, attitudes and behaviour to bring us more in line with the transformed level of humanness which is God's greatest desire for us.

Listening skills

The way we listen is a vital and significant contribution to the communication process. By effective listening, conflict situations can sometimes be avoided; they can often be improved.

If listening skills are measured by the ability to answer questions accurately, politicians come low down on the scale of listening effectiveness. A study of eight television interviews conducted during the 1987 British election campaign revealed that Prime Minister Margaret Thatcher and opposition leader Neil Kinnock evaded more than half the questions put to them. Thirty-one different ways of evasion were analysed in Mrs Thatcher's 56 per cent and Mr Kinnock's 59 per cent apparent inability to hear or respond to the questions asked. (Survey by Dr Peter Bull and Kate Mayer quoted in Sir Robin Day,

Grand Inquisitor, Weidenfeld & Nicolson, 1989.)

The thirty-one different ways of evading the questions were grouped together into eleven main types which included: ignoring the question; acknowledging the question without answering; questioning the answer; attacking the questioner; attacking the interviewer; declining the answer; scoring points off political opponents; giving an incomplete answer; repeating a previous answer; and claiming to have already answered the question. No wonder people say that politicians don't listen!

How well do you listen? Most of us think we listen attentively, effectively and with full understanding.

Listening competence

Research in the United States reveals that in working situations, where there should be a high commitment to productive listening, the average listening competence is only 25 per cent of maximum effectiveness. This implies that three-quarters of what we hear, or think we hear, is ignored, forgotten, distorted, or totally misunderstood. At a purely economic level this is cause for serious concern, for it needs no skill in maths to work out what would happen in a large company if through poor listening each employee made a one-hundred-pound error a year. At an annual rate, a company of five thousand workers would be losing half a million pounds. When poor and ineffectual listening is considered at the non-economic level of work, family life and other relationships a different kind of cost is involved, a cost whose effects can be far more serious and destructive than purely financial concerns.

Welcome home

William rushed in the door. He was expecting a welcoming party. Maybe Jane was in the kitchen making supper for the children? William called out, but there was no reply.

He was tired from the flight. Having to wait practically half an hour for a taxi was an added frustration. When you expect to see your wife with the car ready for you after a week of gruelling meetings in those dusty Far Eastern towns and cities, it's just about the top-up level for stress and dissatisfaction when no one turns up to meet you.

'I'm back.'

Still no sound. When William gets his coat off and pounds into the kitchen, Jane is standing with her back to the door.

'Hello.'

'I thought you were coming to meet me . . . Where are the children, I would have thought you'd have them ready to greet me . . . Haven't you got anything ready for supper?'

'The children are at your mother's. And I am afraid I have to go out to a parent-teacher meeting.'

'But what about me? I was expecting to see you at the station. Anyway you knew when I was coming back. I told you.'

William was right. He *had* told Jane about his trip, the dates, the times, the whole itinerary. But Jane has reached a point in her life where things go in one ear and out the other. It has something to do with the pressures of looking after the house and family, and trying to hold down an unsatisfactory part-time job. Jane actually thought that William had been inconsiderate and uncaring, arriving back without at least phoning to tell her. She was cross when she heard him come in. In fact, she'd like to have arranged the lift, the children, the meal and everything to please. Jane found herself in as much turmoil about it all as William. Both were hurt. It had happened before and it would happen again.

Listening and conflict management

Jane and William *both* need to change. Conversations always have two sides. Poor communication has its faults at both ends, even though some may need to do more work in adjusting their level of skills than others. Jane's need is obvious. She needs to listen more attentively. William's need is plain, too. He needs to communicate more clearly.

The way we listen

What happens in everyday listening? Do we really hear as much as we think we hear? The fact is, we simply cannot listen to everything which happens in detail all around us. We have neither the time, the full spectrum of attention nor the necessary concentration to take in every word, sound, or nuance of aural activity. Listening is like the reading skills we exercise with a daily newspaper. Something may catch our eye immediately and we exclude everything else as we take in the matter which interests us. We may scan the entire paper, turning over its pages quickly to evaluate its contents. We then may focus in on small blocks of information, scanning, evaluating, then giving precise attention to the smallest features.

The way we use our ears is not dissimilar to our eyes. In listening we hear, select and then interpret what our minds register of the sounds around us. Certain levels of communication like a shout, or some other matter of particular interest, may cause us to give extra concentration. A person's body language may stimulate our attention, too, as they lean towards us, imparting some significant or even secret thought for our ears only. We, too, may lean our head towards them. We may cup a hand to our ear. We even talk about 'keeping our ears open' for matters of particular concern or interest, implying that our listening system closes down to some degree in certain less stimulating circumstances, like a dull meeting, or with someone whose endless stream of conversation simply bores the pants off us. All this reminds us that listening is a voluntary activity, and we only hear and register what we choose to hear.

- Next time you can stand or sit still in a public place for a few minutes, try listening to all the sounds around you. Listen in general to everything that is going on, scanning the space you are in for every available sound experience.
- Now select some particular sound. It may be a conversation or some other activity. You may choose. Concentrate for at least five minutes, keeping your eyes open.
- Do the same exercise with your eyes closed and see what difference this makes.
- What range of sounds did you discover?
- Did your concentration wander?
- Was there any difference in hearing between open and shut eyes?
- Which sounds are the easiest to bring back to your memory now, and why?

Improving hearing

People often comment with approval on what they describe as a good listener. To listen well is to accept the personhood of the speaker, contributing to his or her sense of self-worth by indicating that what he has to say is worth listening to. Enhanced listening skills bring an important resource to conflict management for both prevention and relief of friction. How can you improve your general ability to hear with accuracy?

- Ask some members of your family, or some friends or colleagues to tell you how they rate you on the

NEW WAYS TO RESPOND 183

listening scale. Would they describe the way they perceive you as a listener as intense, attentive, interested, satisfactory, sometimes inattentive, often lacking concentration, bored, in another world altogether!
- Ask your friends to say what subjects, situations or conditions they have noticed 'turn you off'.
- Ask them how they observe from your body language when your concentration is failing (e.g. quality of eye contact, glazed eyes, drooping shoulders, looking away . . .)
- Ask if the weaker side of your listening ability is evident in any other particular ways, such as mannerisms, bad habits and nervous tics.
- Ask for examples to back up these observations.

Learning the lessons

To learn from these exercises, try setting yourself an action plan. An action plan means assigning yourself some manageable goals for each day and keeping a note of your progress. It doesn't matter if the progress you make is modest, so long as you aim to make strides in the right direction. What should you note, and what practical aims should you have?

- Some people have physical hearing difficulties and never realise it. It may be wise to have your hearing checked if you have any doubts. Even the heavy build-up of wax can dull sensation, making hearing difficult and imprecise and concentration poor.
- Do you listen fully to others without interrupting? Are you the kind of person who never lets another person finish a sentence because you have jumped ahead of them in your mind? Maybe you are always filling in the gaps in another person's conversation, always supplying the missing words or phrases?

- Are you a wanderer? Does your mind wander down all kinds of paths, except that of the speaker? Do you daydream when talking to others?
- Do you get distracted? Do the conversations of others, or other sounds and sights easily distract you from what you should be hearing?
- Do you fail to ask for clarification or repetition when you do not grasp what has been said?
- Do you feel embarrassed to show that you do not understand particular words which have been used, and therefore fail to ask for explanation?
- Do you unwittingly pretend to know about matters to which the speaker refers, to give the impression you possess more knowledge than you do? Does your failure to ask for further explanation hinder your comprehension?
- Do you back off people you don't like or find difficult in some way, failing to give the attention, encouragement, and worth which you would advance to those closer to you?
- Do you get bored? (Be honest!) How does your boredom and frustration communicate itself? Do you look around, hop from one foot to another, and make impatient grunts or half-formed comments to try and wind things up quickly?
- Do you usually make statements when you have ideas about someone else's behaviour, work or thinking? Or do you ask questions drawing the other person out and letting them express their ideas to you?
- If you attend meetings with others, are you a listener or a talker? What could you do to improve the active or passive quality of your contributions?
- Now work out manageable goals for yourself on these matters, giving yourself a timetable for the exercise.
- Note your progress. Be brave. Don't be over-hard on yourself. Aim for improvement. Take pleasure in the small but significant changes you are able to make.

Sensed and seen

One of the reasons that these listening skills are so essential is that communication is about the transference of messages from one party to another. The words and body language which accompany them need the co-operation of the hearer to ensure that the message is capable of accurate interpretation. A message is both sensed and seen. One study shows that our communication is 55 per cent non-verbal, 38 per cent vocal inflection and only 7 per cent words!

So if my eyes are wandering when I should be listening to something of some personal importance to the speaker, the speaker may sense this, becoming inwardly alarmed, not only risking the distortion of the message, but also receiving a negative communication in return. He or she may think me distant, disinterested or perhaps uncaring. I may not wish to give this impression at all, but bad listening habits have said it all for me.

If I interrupt unnecessarily, I may risk jumping to conclusions. I can fail to give myself time to evaluate the evidence of what is being said. On the other hand, I may veer to the other extreme. I may be determined to listen to every word, yet sit dumbly and unresponsively without question, comment or signs of comprehension or approbation. When that is the case my contribution in the reciprocal communication process can go badly wrong.

Active listening skills

There are several ways to help the person who is speaking. All of us have a need to be listened to and understood. And the way we perceive that listening and understanding are in progress takes place as much with our eyes as with what our ears hear subsequently. The way our active listening skills come over will convince the speaker of our below-surface attitudes and can make a great deal of difference in the assessment of our sincerity, integrity and maturity. In particular **this** lends strength to verbal interplay where conflict is evident. Here are some areas for practice.

- Concentrate on the dominant theme of the speaker's communication.
- Ask questions for clarification. Reflect back what you are hearing, both to show understanding and encourage further disclosure. This shows your concern to understand deeply what the speaker is saying.
- Don't interrupt unless you have to.
- Use your eyes and other bodily gestures in natural ways to back up your understanding of what is being said. Beware of your negative non-verbal listening responses like looking at your watch or gazing around. Watch your mannerisms and try to eliminate anything distracting like fidgeting, frowning or fiddling.
- Smiling can help if it is unforced and natural. Do you let your face and features be mobile and expressive?
- What do your eyes say? Are they dead and lifeless, concentrated and concerned, warm and smiling?
- Tune in to the speaker's mood. Try to understand his or her feelings, what is going on behind the words and anything left unsaid which your antennae are meant to pick up (or not). Listen to the tone of voice and any variations of pitch or pace.

Conflicts and arguments

The following guidelines may be helpful during arguments and conflicts.

- If you are in an argument, make up your mind to stay cool under all circumstances. Don't rise to the

bait of taunts and accusations. Don't rush in with your responses. Be patient, hear the person out, and stick to the subject.
- During arguments, it is even more important to have the sensation you have been listened to. Pay especial attention to all that is being said. Speak slowly, and try and ask questions which will elicit a rational response.
- Remember that feelings not only run high, but feelings are at stake. It may be at least as important as the issue itself that the feelings it has generated are properly appreciated, and acknowledged as acceptable. So where appropriate, ask questions about the feelings too, like 'What did you feel about that?', 'How do you feel now?', 'Can you tell me who you are angry with or who you blame?', and so on.
- Try and see the other person's point of view. Don't try and score points, but try and remove the sting by offering a reasonable explanation or a solution workable to both sides.
- Know what makes you angry and work on ways of defusing your anger should your anger response be triggered suddenly by the argument in hand.
- In a fight a cat's fur bristles and the claws are ready. Someone may have put your back up, but you are a rational creature. Take a few deep breaths. Ask God to keep you steady. And remember who and what you are.

Standing up for yourself

Some people, of course, far from rising to the bait where an argument is concerned, actually run away from it. Some of us can't stand conflict. We are not spoiling for a fight, we are fleeing from it. This talk of conciliation in arguments is all very well, but what if you happen to be made the other way round? You are the person who keeps the peace at all costs. You will pay any price not to have the waters muddied. In fact, peace is the problem.

Nice guy

Sandy is a nice guy. That's what everyone says about him. He even looks the part. Fair hair, blue eyes, medium height, slim build. Sandy is a computer programmer and sits in front of his PC every day in a software house in the London suburbs. Sandy plays snooker at weekends, goes to church on Sundays, and has lots of friends and is well liked. He is one of those people you never see angry. Not on the surface, anyway.

Sandy knows about computers. When his church wanted to computerise, Sandy was the obvious person to ask. The church sought his guidance, and he came up with the goods, a very suitable package for their needs. Of course, Sandy knew where to buy as well. When you are in the business, it's not difficult to find the lowest prices. Sandy went off to London's West End and came back with hardware and software and installed them all successfully.

A few weeks' later, Sandy received a call. The computer at the church had broken down. Later that night, Sandy discovered a serious electrical fault in the central processing unit. The main board had blown. But when Sandy informed the dealers, they were adamant. 'Sorry, sir, nothing we can do. That model was ex-demonstration. It was sold as seen. If it's faulty we'll repair it, but we'll have to charge you.'

Sandy knew this was unjust. He also knew it was untrue. There had never been a single word to him about an 'as-seen' sale. But he found himself shaking inside. He smiled at the salesman, who wasn't smiling back. He started to splutter out something about guarantees and unmerchantable quality, but he couldn't bear a fight. They put it right while he waited. It's a throw-away industry. Out with one part, in with another. But it can be an expensive procedure. Sandy paid the bill out of his own pocket. It was the best part of a whole week's wages. So much for the bargain.

The church administrator was delighted to see the computer back in place. Smiling warmly at Sandy as he went out the door, she offered the comment, 'The quality of service you get in the West End is tremendous, isn't it.' Sandy nodded. The computer worked fine after that. No more problems. Everybody says what a nice person Sandy is. It is not the first time he has sidestepped a dispute and ended up paying the bill.

Feeling fearful

There are many reasons why some find standing up for themselves difficult to cope with. In every case fear is involved. That fear may have something to do with inner insecurities like fear of failure, emotional hurt or rejection. We looked at our early life experiences in Part One, and saw how they set the stage for our development into adulthood. But whatever the reasons for the way we feel about ourselves, the fact is we should not let our feelings necessarily run our lives. Feelings are an unreliable guide to reality, and an equally deceitful mentor when it comes to dealing with conflict. Those who automatically flare up, spoiling for a fight, are just as much at fault as those who run fast and furiously in the opposite direction. There is a difference between being meek and being frightened.

Blocked feelings

Sandy kicked himself again and again for not making his thoughts plain at the computer dealers. After all, he knows his business. But he let them get away with it. His girlfriend, Caroline, in a moment of unusual frankness told him bluntly, 'They saw you coming, Sandy.'

Sandy knew what she meant. When conflict arises he backs off. His head goes forward, he starts to shake it slowly from side to side. His mind is saying no to the situation, but he blocks his reaction. The dealer saw him bite his lip. Sandy wasn't going to fight back. Instinctively the dealer knew it. He took advantage because he knew he would get away with it. And he did.

Push-over

If you are the kind of person who finds self-assertion difficult, you may well end up in conflict with others because you are a push-over, you are an easy person to take advantage of. The conflict may be felt because you cannot easily say no. You have learned that doing what other people want brings acceptance and esteem. Maybe you are the kind of person who likes to be known as the one whose door is always open; or the one who will help at any time of the day or night; someone for whom nothing is too much trouble. All that is highly laudable. But what are your hidden motives?

Does fear of rejection play a significant part? Do you ever find times when your drive towards acceptance by others places an immense stress and strain upon your ability to fulfil all the tasks you have in hand? Do you wish you could blow the whistle on someone else's expectations of you, but do not have the inner grit to do so — you'd rather run in the opposite direction?

If you are like this, then don't despair. We are all made differently and have to learn to cope with the more awkward elements of our makeup. Some people undergo assertiveness training to help them out of this kind of difficulty. Whereas such training has its value under certain circumstances, discovering skills to become suddenly assertive may make you into a more unpleasant person altogether. It doesn't take much skill to be stubborn, pushy, or aggressive, whoever you are and however passive you may consider yourself. Like an angry bull, you put your head down, shut your eyes, and aim furiously and unforgivingly at your target. If you have been told you need to learn to assert yourself more, then be aware of the importance of risk taking.

All change

If Sandy could rewind his story and play back his encounter at the computer store using a different set of reactions altogether, what might he change? Before he gets there he needs to have decided in his mind not only what the problem is with the goods he is returning, but what he considers to be fair and just with regard to the dealer's responsibility in the matter. If he suspects there might be a tussle, then he should be ready (a) to face up to the need to argue his case; and (b) to be prepared to deal with his own inner reactions.

Sandy's case was simple. The goods as supplied were faulty, and probably were so from the point of sale. The vendor's responsibility under consumer law is to replace or repair. The dealer had sold the goods as suitable for the task for which Sandy was applying them at the church.

Childhood memories

Sandy's reaction was more complex. Ever since he was a child his mother had told him that he must 'be nice' under all circumstances. If he ever became cross, agitated, or tearful, the response was always the same. 'You must be nice.' When Sandy wasn't nice, and showed his true feelings, his mother would vent her displeasure and Sandy would suffer in some way as a result. Sandy now copes by being nice to everyone. It guarantees security, friendship and, more importantly for him, absence of rejection. The only thing is, as Caroline pointed out, he frequently gets walked over.

Risk taking

So to modify his behaviour Sandy needs to learn to take a risk. He doesn't need to become more assertive in the sense that he shouts louder, threatens more, and introduces snarling grimaces into his store of facial expressions. Sandy needs to make up his mind that he will put his feelings to one side and press his case, politely but firmly. After all, even if he were to lose the esteem of the computer dealer, what would that matter? It is a simple matter of justice.

But a risk *is* involved. Something serious is at stake in denying inner drives which have little validity or correspondence with truth, but which have reigned unchallenged and supreme all your adult life. Something serious is at stake in denying an action to someone else which is of importance to them.

Changed ways

When Sandy went back to the very same dealer a year later because a disk drive which he'd purchased had similarly gone wrong, he was better prepared.

'I'll be grateful if you can help me. You remember I bought this drive here last week. It's never worked properly. It's making a lot of noise and sometimes won't read the disks I put into it. I'd like you to exchange it please.'

The dealer grimaced slightly. 'It was all right when you took it away from here. I'll get it repaired for you. But I am afraid we can't guarantee goods like this.'

Sandy felt himself begin to shake slightly. So he took a deep breath and with it took two decisions. He would not listen to the voice now beginning to wail inside him, 'Be nice, be nice', and he would speak slowly and firmly and not run to the other extreme of being cross and confrontational.

Sandy smiled purposefully at the dealer. 'I am sorry I must insist you either change it or give me my money back. I dispute that the goods were working when I bought them from you since you were unable to give me a working demonstration when asked. I suggest the disk drive was of unmerchantable quality, and I must ask you to exchange it or refund my money.'

The dealer paused for a moment. 'I'll see if I can get it repaired for you. But I don't know when you'll get it back.'

Sandy took another deep intake of breath. He spoke quietly, firmly and clearly, 'I am sorry. I will not accept that. If you cannot replace it, I'll have to ask you to refund my cash payment in full.'

'I'll see if we've got another one . . .'

Learning to overcome

Sandy overcame a habit of a lifetime. But it meant taking a significant risk with his own feelings and with the reactions of the dealer concerned.

- If you are the kind of person who is not naturally good at standing up for yourself, what kinds of risk should you be learning to take?
- What cherished inner drives and feelings do you need to learn to ignore?
- What kind of under-surface fears matter greatly to you?
- How do those fears affect the way you respond positively or negatively to conflict?
- In what ways have you noticed that others get the better of you or take unfair advantage? Think of situations where you have sidestepped conflict but have reaped the disadvantage of not fully contesting some proposed action or behaviour.
- Choose one of those situations, and in the safety of your mind, examine all possible ways you might have responded.
- Which of those ways would you recommend to someone else in your situation and why?
- Do you need to take the risk to counteract the way that others may manipulate or blackmail you into unwanted ways of response? Do you need to learn to deny tactics

such as feigned aggressive resistance, floods of tears, and expressions of mild domestic violence such as breaking dishes, physical gestures and other forms of emotional manipulation? The longer you let yourself be swayed by such exercises of emotion, the more you will be manipulated.
- Do you need to believe more clearly that God cares about issues of truth and justice, and by running away from such issues you express your own unwitting complicity in these matters?
- Do you need to trust more actively that if you seek to honour God in situations like these and in questions of truth, justice and integrity, he will uphold you?
- What wrong, untrusting attitudes do you need to repent?

Coping strategies

Whether you find conflict drives you wild or drives you away, we all have to learn to cope with conflict situations maturely and as Christians. In the gospels we constantly see Jesus in situations of conflict. We can learn from his responses.

- Jesus was a superb listener who took in not only words but the thoughts being expressed *beneath* the words. His encounter with Nicodemus (John 3:1–21) is a fine example of reading between the lines and perceiving the deeper question being asked.
- Jesus was not afraid of anger, but his anger was always controlled and in proportion to the issue concerned. We see him angry, but never fuming, explosive or boiling over.
- Jesus did not back away from situations of conflict. He welcomed conflict as a positive opportunity to teach the truth.

NEW WAYS TO RESPOND

- Jesus enhanced the principle of justice enshrined in the law ('an eye for an eye, a tooth for a tooth') with his injunction to turn the other cheek (Matt. 5:38–42). The principle of justice had been misinterpreted as a law of retaliation. Jesus was outlawing revenge and reprisal. His priority was forgiveness and pardon.
- Jesus found his disciples infuriating on occasions, with their slowness to learn and 'little faith'. He was, however, always patient with them. He learned to accept their weaknesses, and 'dust round' the impetuosity of Peter and the frailties of the other disciples. When you decide to accept a person and not to be irritated and enraged by their failings, you have time to perceive and appreciate the value of their personality and strengths.
- We hear on a number of occasions that Jesus withdrew from the crowds when conflict developed. We may conclude that he was sensitive to when others had become hot-headed, and no more could be achieved by rational discussion.
- Jesus was 'despised and rejected' (Isa. 53:3) yet the constant spiritual, emotional and physical battering he received never once deflected him from his overall task and all the necessary conflicts he was involved in.
- When the moment came for Jesus to suffer he did not shirk the pain. 'As a sheep before her shearers is silent, so he did not open his mouth' (Isa. 53:7).
- In a practical way what can you learn from Jesus's method of coping with conflict?
- Can you think of specific attitudes and characteristics which will make a difference to you in your present situation?

Facing up to change

No one in human history ever faced a period of more deeply sustained conflict than Jesus Christ. What is so deeply impressive is the quality of peace and stability which comes shining through the pages of the gospels as we see Jesus moving from one situation of strife to another. We see him listening deeply and intently to the woman at the well. We observe him fearlessly facing the Pharisees' bigotry and wrong teaching. We see him patiently working around the disciples' weaknesses, accepting them with love. And even with Judas, Jesus controls his response, accepting quietly what must be done. Paul uses Jesus as a model of exemplary human behaviour, and calls for changes which reflect the qualities of Jesus we have just been considering. Those changes have much to do with how Paul counsels his readers to cope with conflict.

> If you have any encouragement from being united with Christ, if any comfort from his love, if any fellowship with the Spirit, if any tenderness and compassion, then make my joy complete by being like-minded, having the same love, being one in spirit and purpose. Do nothing out of selfish ambition or vain conceit, but in humility consider others better than yourselves. Each of you should look not only to your own interests, but also to the interests of others. Your attitude should be the same as that of Christ Jesus (Phil. 2:1–5).

9

NEW ATTITUDES TO LEARN

Conflict arises as much from bad habits as it does from bad relationships. We all have our habits of mind, speech and behaviour. They lend distinctiveness to our personalities and colour to our lives and friendships. Many habits are innocuous.

Sheila is adamant. She will not be seen outside the house without her lipstick on. Norman is cautious. Suggest an outing to him, he'll need a good half an hour turning it over before he'll ever make up his mind. Joanna likes her routine. She must have her marmalade at breakfast or the day can't start.

Routine living

We are all creatures of habit to a greater or lesser extent. Routines of some sort are good for us. It's the way we organise the more private parts of our day. Getting up, preparing for bed; the way we wash, morning exercises, a hot drink, a book at bedtime, turning out the light, even counting sheep! In some form, all these routines are a common part of everyone's experience. They help us manage the transitions from one day to another when our brains are tired and need to run down gently as we prepare to enter or emerge from sleep. Violate your sleeping and waking patterns by too many late nights, too many personal concerns, too much burning of the midnight oil for college or for work, then your routines quickly slip out of the window. The result is a growing feeling of discomfort. Routines matter. Some habits are to be greatly valued for they protect our well-being. But habits are jealous creatures. They do not like to be neglected, stood up, or jettisoned.

Habitual responses

In essence, there is nothing wrong with habits. Habits can be good and bad. What concerns us now is how bad habits can affect relationships. We are not talking about arguments over who has the last scraping of the marmalade. Habits of mind, speech and behaviour can have far deeper effects on the way people respond to each other. Deep-seated anxieties, profound feelings of guilt, aggressively confrontational use of language, unrelieved stress patterns, unforgiving attitudes, suspicions, bitterness and grudges, all contribute significantly to conflict in relationships. Habits are not something you catch like the flu. They are learned. They are ways of habitual response, often unconsciously absorbed and practised from our earliest years onwards.

- Can you think of any significant habits of mind, speech or behaviour which cause problems in your relationships?
- Why do you think you respond in this way?
- Ask someone close to you, a friend or member of the family, if they have observed that you respond negatively in any predictable manner given a certain set of circumstances.
- From what they know of you, do they have any explanation for your responses?

NEW ATTITUDES TO LEARN

The anxiety response

Gini and Bob celebrated their diamond wedding last Easter. It would have been a truly splendid time if Bob had not been taken ill on the Sunday morning. They'd had a large family party the night before which had gone really well. Bob had looked a little tired even then, but he had a good night. It wasn't until after breakfast that he started to feel the chest pains. It was pretty uncomfortable. He insisted it was just indigestion. Too much rich food and drink. But Bob's brother drove him to Casualty. The doctor suggested keeping him in overnight for some tests. And sure enough, Bob had suffered a mild heart attack.

The hospital staff were marvellous, and Bob was properly cared for and given plenty of help and information about diet and exercise to help him live as full a life as possible. The consultant said he should do well and suggested Bob should lose a few pounds, cut down on cholesterol and take a good long walk each day.

Bob has been in great shape ever since. It's Gini who has suffered. Gini is in good health, too, apart from her blood pressure which has a tendency to rise when she gets herself all knotted up. And that is exactly what has happened over Bob's illness. You can tell her otherwise, but Gini is convinced that Bob's life is in grave danger. She's terrified that he'll have another attack. That he'll be all on his own, and that will be it.

It's understandable to be concerned. But Bob *is* doing well. The doctor said he'd be fine from now on. The loss of a stone in weight has helped a great deal. Gini's pleased, but under the surface pooh-poohs what's said. She's terrified of being left alone. 'What would happen to me? I'd never be able to cope. I haven't got a clue how to manage household bills or tax or anything like that. And what about the loneliness? I just can't stand the thought of it.'

Dr Robson, their family doctor, smiled at Gini. 'You're living in the future, Gini. Tomorrow can take care of itself.

But we're not there yet. So why not get on with today?'

'Yes, but you don't understand. If I'm not careful with him now, he might have another attack. You admit he could have another one, don't you? I'm not making it up am I?' Gini was breathing deeply, her brow furrowed, her face betraying a look of acute concern.

Dr Robson was patient with her. 'I did say there's a *possibility* of another attack. But frankly, he is doing so well, I don't expect it. I have to tell you, though, if you continue to exert the pressure on him that you are doing, you do risk adversely affecting his health. All your worrying affects Bob too. It causes stress, and that's just what you want to aim to avoid, Gini.'

The talk with the GP helped for a day or so. Gini certainly felt more cheerful afterwards. But she continued to worry. It was a cause of some considerable conflict, with several practical implications. Gini wouldn't let Bob use the car on his own in case 'he came over funny'. She wouldn't let him go to the pool on Saturday mornings for his early morning swim. She even got worried about his going shopping on his own.

Bob was furious. 'Look, Gini, this is getting past a joke. I'm fit. Didn't Dr Robson tell you that? I can drive. I can walk. I can swim. I'm not an invalid. Stop treating me as though I'm ready for the grave. Just stop all this worrying. Look on the bright side. You don't need to worry you know. I'm fine and I don't need you to bury me before my time.'

That did it. Gini went up in smoke. 'You don't understand how I worry about you. I lie in bed thinking of you night after night. I even dream about what might occur. And sometimes I wake up in a panic thinking I've heard the front-door bell and that something's happened.'

Bob tried to hold his frustration back. He took a deep breath and spoke slowly and kindly. 'Well it's about time you learned that adage about giving no thought for the morrow, my love. Why can't we enjoy today? There's so much to live for.'

Gini was feeling muzzy-headed. She wanted to lie down. She knew that Bob was right in some ways. But how could she change? She'd always been like this, almost since she was a child. 'Maybe I'm just the worrying sort.' Gini decided she would heed the doctor's word and keep quiet for a while. She went and lay down. But it made no difference to her thoughts. They would simply not go away.

Fearful feelings

Anxiety is concerned with our fears. Many anxieties are normal and natural. We all become concerned when a loved one sustains a serious and life-threatening illness. At work, the threat of redundancy, a change of boss, a promotion or an outside job offer, all bring endless possibilities for thought and concern. But spontaneous anxiety and deep-seated fears are not the same. The problem with anxiety is that it can easily distort the truth of a situation. It may cause us seriously to consider all kinds of things, which if not *beyond* possibility are beyond *reasonable* possibility, at least for the time being.

Gini is like that. Her projections go beyond the reasonable and likely. The potency of her fears drive her to live not in the present, but in the future. And, of course, in the future, anything can happen because we are not there yet. So the distortions which fear loves to feed on can have their full rein in any kind of situation where a future setting is being contemplated.

Fear drives us into the corner. We feel disarmed and helpless. The feeling of helplessness is extremely unsettling. Deep down it reminds us of feeling abandoned in early childhood. 'Where's Mummy . . . Where's Daddy?' We may not remember the situations, but our emotions don't forget. And these kinds of archetypal fear are within all of us. The real issue is, have we learned to master our fears? These are powerful emotions, and if we do not learn to master them, they will seek to master us.

Worries about the worst

The kinds of fear we are thinking about often stem from deeply engrained habits of mind. How do you react when there is some unexpected news? The telephone goes, at the other end you hear the voice of a friend or relative with whom you have not been in contact for a couple of years.

- Do you immediately think the worst?
- Do you listen quietly and steadily till they have explained the reason for their call?
- Do you assume if something is wrong you'll face up to it when you know what it is?

Some people immediately think the worst in any and every situation. If you are like that yourself, you probably find yourself in a regular state of worry and dread. The worst state is when you effectively respond to each situation with the question, 'What if . . . the worst happened . . .'.

Conflicts of love

If the question 'what if' continually comes to mind, you need to be convinced that however you have obtained it, you are in the possession of a bad habit. Unknowingly you have practised it faithfully over the years in all kinds of situations. You probably have not suffered silently. Others will not only have lent an initially sympathetic ear to your troubles, but will have been drawn into your pains and misfortunes.

Anxiety and love are often closely joined. Fears are directed towards those dear to us. These conflicts of love involve a powerful desire that others will fall in with your desires or concerns. Such concerns show in a desire for control. Gini wanted to control all Bob's choices to lessen the impact of her own inner fears and dread. Such unconscious desire to manipulate is a coping strategy of this kind of anxiety. It's a shortcut solution. I find myself anxious about someone. The quick solution is to force them to surrender to the whim of my anxiety. The long-term and more costly way is to modify my own reaction.

Imagine a situation of anxiety concerning someone you love. At the onset, what changes do you notice in yourself and in the way you are likely to respond to them and the situation?

- Do you long to be in control?
- Do you consciously or unconsciously try and manipulate situations and people?
- Do you become tactless? Do your concerns and worries occasion the kinds of verbal short cuts which come out in bluntness and even outright confrontation?
- Do you interfere?
- Do you get heated?
- Do you find that much of your motivation happens unconsciously?

Uncovering fear

What are your deep-down fears? We are not talking about the little worries we all have like having a tooth drilled, unexpected bills, and whether the garden fence will survive the next storm. Deep-down fears have much to do with dread. Dread is that deeply unsettling emotion which makes us feel horribly off colour. It's that sickening feeling, that inner sense of foreboding and disaster which we all dislike so much. Take a moment of quiet and write down the answers to these questions.

- What is your greatest fear?
- Is there anything in your past which has invested that matter with such great power for you?
- What other fears are important for you?
- Have you any insight into the origins of these fears?
- Can you think of any ways in which these fears have emerged and affected your relationships with anyone else?

Fear is the attitude of dread we have fixed within us. Anxiety is the extension of fear. When those fears come to the surface, they then become the powerful and unsettling emotions which feed on the inner uncertainties which have, perhaps for years, been ticking away inside us. Those inner fears are just waiting to be triggered by some external situation which will correspond to the shape of the inner fear. When released, the panic rises to the surface. No wonder others get manipulated in the process. Our fears need to be faced, accepted and dealt with.

Resolving fear

'I don't like to be afraid because it means I may be out of control. I may be helpless. I may not be able to influence the outcome of my life, or the lives of those close to me, or events and situations which matter most to me.' This description of fear brings out an important element in what requires resolution in our fear attitudes.

We do not live in an impersonal universe. There is a loving creator God behind it who longs that we should know the closeness and security of his love. His perfect love drives out fear (1 John 4:18). Jesus said, 'Do not worry about tomorrow, for tomorrow will worry about itself. Each day has enough trouble of its own' (Matt. 6:34). This was said in the context of God's provision as a loving Father.

I tell you, do not worry about your life ... Look at the birds ... they do not sow or reap or store away in barns, and yet your heavenly Father feeds them. Are you not much more valuable than they? ... So do not worry, saying, 'What shall we eat?' or 'What shall we drink?' or 'What shall we wear?' ... your heavenly Father knows that you need them. But seek first his kingdom and his righteousness, and all these things will be given to you as well (Matt. 6:25–33).

The anxiety process

When you have a moment of quiet ask yourself what difference you will let Jesus's words make to the fears you have analysed above. Jesus recognises our human predisposition to anxiety. His words are realistic, but they don't end there. Jesus encourages us to face up to our fears. When he says 'Do not worry about your life ...' he is not arguing with our emotions, he is putting on the brakes. He is saying we must put a stop to the worrying *process*. We are in control of it. Worrying is negative. We chew over a particular concern. We are like a dog with a bone. We will not let go of it. And yet let go of it we must.

Step by step

There are three steps. The first is to believe that God is your heavenly Father and that he is just as Jesus describes him to be. He loves you and wants to help you. He has promised to provide for you. It is easy to say that in a few words, but the meaning and implication are immensely deep. So pause again, and ask yourself seriously:

- Have I really grasped the wonder and security of what it means to know God as my heavenly Father?

The second step involves the kingdom of God. When Jesus says we should 'seek first his kingdom and his righteousness' he is talking about priorities and commitments. The kingdom of God is his rule in the world and in your life. His righteousness is the quality of life he desires for you. So now think about where you are going with God:

- Have I come to the point where I have let God rule actively in my life?
- Am I in consequence going to live as one dedicated to God's standards of behaviour, including the management of my inner thoughts and concerns?

The third step involves being prepared to hand over to God your present worries and the stock of fears and dread which underlies them. Then Jesus says you must *stop* worrying. You must understand that this is as practical as being told to stop scratching your nose! Every time we are tempted to worry, we must learn to exercise a little discipline.

The discipline for anxiety is to reject the steps to anticipating the worst. Every time an anxious thought comes to mind, let it go. Decide now *not* to chew it over. As soon as you catch yourself thinking, 'What if . . . ' stop the process in mid flight. Don't let yourself slip back into the bad habits of negative meditation.

- Take some moments to hand over your deepest fears and concerns to God.
- Repent of your lack of trust in the God who loves you and understands all your needs.
- Believe in his promise to provide for your life.
- Spend some moments speaking quietly to God in your own words about what you have discovered about yourself and your need to be freed from anxiety and fear.

Bearing grudges

Bernard and Marcia were in a quandary. Marcia's sister, Beryl, had just died. They weren't a large family and naturally they all wanted to be together at such a time. But Bernard hadn't talked to Dick, Beryl's husband, for about four or five years.

They'd been the best of friends until then. It all happened when Bernard asked Dick for some financial advice. Dick had put some money into a few oil shares which had done rather well. He thought that Bernard should have a go too, which Bernard did, investing several thousands in the company, which subsequently ran into trouble. Bernard lost some of his capital, but was horrified beyond measure when he discovered that Dick had got his own money out just in time. Bernard was appalled because Dick had not made any attempt to warn or contact him. When Dick explained that his money was managed by a broker on his behalf, he was not listened to with any sympathy. Bernard considered his brother-in-law had betrayed him. It was worse than a family insult. A member of the family had done the dirty on him.

This led to tremendous conflict. There were, of course, the initial encounters. Bernard wasn't prepared to admit that Dick was no more a financial expert than he was. Dick was very sorry: sorry that Bernard had lost money; sorry that he hadn't given better advice; sorry that he had ever shown any enthusiasm for Clarkson Oil in the first place.

'I *am* sorry, Bernard, but you simply cannot hold me responsible for the oil company's failure. As for tipping you off, I knew no more than you did. My broker manages my funds. I never hear till the end of the quarter what he's been up to.'

But hold him responsible, Bernard did. Poor Beryl. It was of immense distress to her. Marcia secretly wonders whether all the stress and turmoil had anything to do with the cancer which Beryl contracted only a matter of months afterwards. It made Marcia all the more angry with Bernard when he deliberated over going back to the house after the service.

'What – go back to Dick's house! You must be joking, Marcia. After all he's done to me . . .'

'He's done nothing to you, Bernard. You lost a few pounds on the stock market. You've blamed it all on Dick when it was just as much your own silly fault for not taking professional financial advice. You've split the family over it. You probably made Beryl ill in the first place. And now you won't even honour my sister's memory by entering her home. What kind of person are you?'

As it turned out, Bernard and Marcia did go back to the house. But Dick and Bernard still didn't hit it off. Dick tried but Bernard was determined to be awkward despite the circumstances. He offered the bare minimum in courtesies, embarrassing Marcia as well as Edwina and Thomas, their grown-up children.

In the car afterwards, Marcia broke the silence.

'Will you never learn, Bernard? Are you so proud you can't drop your high-minded, self-satisfied pride? My sister is dead. And you have to persist in your grudge against Dick. I don't understand you, Bernard. I simply do not understand you. Why are you so bitter? Why can't you forgive?'

Unforgiveness

Unforgiving attitudes are at the root of many interpersonal conflicts. Children who won't forgive parents. Parents who won't forgive children. Unforgiving husbands and wives. Friends who fall out. Neighbours who don't and won't speak to each other. Whole families at war within themselves or with other families. The longer it goes on the more difficult it is to drop the charge.

Yet the impact that bitterness and grudges lend to conflict in relationships is considerable. Many of us have

NEW ATTITUDES TO LEARN

strongly held feelings. Some of those feelings may be justified. At least there is some basis for the judgment that we have been wronged. But are we right to continue to bear a grudge in this way?

The same habit of mind which is involved with anxiety, the continuing harking back to old fears and dreads is at work here. Unwillingness to forgive is like a habit of mind. We meditate on old hurts, long past. From them we derive some sense of self-righteousness and justification. We think it's our job to punish and re-educate by our vigorous refusal to readmit our adversary to our realm. Yet all these attitudes achieve is conflict. Conflict within me. And conflict within the lives of those associated with me and those with whom I have been embattled.

- Are you involved in an ongoing conflict like this?
- Who is it you are unwilling to forgive?
- How would you put into words the emotions they or their actions evoke in you?
- What is it you find so difficult to forgive and why?

Anger and violence

Unforgiveness and the bitterness it inspires often end up in violence of some sort. Sometimes, there is a fine line which separates acceptable expressions of anger and the uncontrollable boiling over of rage and hostility. Wherever we live in the world, we see the unpleasant outcome of unforgiving and begrudging attitudes in appalling criminal behaviour motivated by hate and loathing.

Before we look at ways of resolving hate, loathing and fixed and unremitting attitudes of unforgiveness we need to go deeper still into human motivation. The existence of overt violence within our society gives us clues to what characterises our human makeup that we should be capable of such destructive attitudes and behaviour.

Whether it is an obscene crime like the IRA's attempt to wipe out the British Tory cabinet in the bombing of the Grand Hotel in Brighton; the massacre of students in Tiananmen Square in China; or the slaughter of blacks in the Sharpeville township of South Africa, crimes of hate and loathing take place daily in every part of the world.

In the United Kingdom the general crime rate is approaching 4 million crimes a year. That's 11,000 crimes a day. Or 450 crimes an hour. General crime figures for 1987 were 6 per cent lower than the previous year. But crimes of *violence* increased by 16.9 per cent. In England, Wales and Scotland, there were 140,916 crimes of violence, and 751 murders. In the United States, in 1985, there were 18,980 murders, and an incredible 1,327,440 violent crimes involving significant or serious personal injury. Many of these crimes are motivated by hatred and bitterness. Their significance cannot be discounted where conflict and its management is being considered.

World in decay

We live in a violent world, yet it is also a world of extraordinary contrasts. The contrast is between good and evil. There is so much serious crime. Yet human beings are also capable of stunning achievements in science and technology, the arts and music, and in the sheer humanity demonstrated by the kind of compassion and charity shown to places like Ethiopia, Bangladesh and the Sudan. There is certainly a dimension of our humanness which speaks of the unselfishness, dignity and ingenuity of man. Human relationships can be wonderfully rich, beautiful and tender. They can also descend into conflict, bitterness, rage, spite and violence.

What is wrong with the world, that what could overall be so splendidly wholesome, worth while and good, is in practice being so badly spoiled and in decay?

The answer to that question is one of the main concerns of the opening chapters of Genesis. It shows man, made as a creature with a spiritual nature, and made to know his Creator. It also reveals the rebellion of man and his fall. From the story of Cain and Abel, we encounter the very antithesis in human nature of what was originally designed to be beautiful, wholesome, worth while and good. The historical narrative of Cain and Abel provides us with the very earliest record of murder and fratricide, and a deep insight into the nature of inner and interpersonal conflict from which we all suffer.

The origins of violent conflict

The term Genesis means origins. The first eleven chapters of Genesis give themselves to this theme, dealing with the origins of creation. Chapter 3 is pivotal for the whole Bible in the way it deals with the fall of man. Understanding our fallen nature is essential for comprehending salvation and the coming of Christ, but it is equally important for understanding the true nature of our humanness. That is why, as Genesis progresses through chapter 4 the subject is no longer the fall, but the *fallenness* of man. Man has already broken his relationship with God. Now we move on to see the *consequences* of that shattered relationship, and in particular how the results of the fall work out in relationships in society.

The creation of the first family is recorded in summary form. Adam and Eve give birth to Cain, the elder child, and then to Abel. We are told that Abel was a shepherd and Cain an arable farmer (cf.Gen. 4:1–2). This is the background to what happens subsequently.

History book

Genesis is a historical book. It deals with real people and real events. But it is not written like a modern textbook on history because the purpose is different. Genesis does not always give precise and exhaustive descriptions of people, places and events. In the first eleven chapters, particularly, the approach is selective, giving only the details we need to know. It is more concerned with the message of history than the minutiae of history.

One theme, one thesis

The major concern of the writer of this part of Genesis is to illustrate an outcome. The very first shattered and broken relationship with God had an immediate and devastating impact on human society. And so we become witnesses to the first murder. The first of many violent crimes throughout history. Crimes like the murder of six million Jews in Nazi concentration camps. The murder of ten million Soviet citizens during the Stalin years. The murder of twenty-six million Chinese during the reign of Mao Tse-tung. The murder of ordinary people like you and me, at the hands of violent, maliciously determined, yet perhaps equally ordinary, people. This is the one theme and thesis which the story of Cain and Abel illustrates.

Cain and Abel both bring offerings to the Lord. Abel's offering is accepted; but not Cain's, the elder brother. Cain is clearly furious. In no time his bitterness, his anger, his resentment, overwhelm him. Then out in the field, Cain attacks his brother and kills him. So takes place the very first murder in the whole of human history.

Unacceptable offerings?

> In the course of time Cain brought some of the fruits of the soil as an offering to the Lord. But Abel brought fat portions from some of the firstborn of his flock. The Lord looked with favour on Abel and his offering, but on Cain and his offering he did not look with favour. So Cain was very angry and his face was downcast (Gen. 4:3–5).

What went wrong at the sacrifice? Why did Abel win approval but Cain find his offering rejected? After all, this is the incident which sparked off Cain's terrible response. Was there something wrong with Cain's offering? That certainly is the easiest conclusion. Abel brought the prescribed offering and Cain did not.

It is a worthy theory. But it is not what the narrative suggests. In fact, God's response to both Cain and Abel had nothing to do with the offering itself. No rules are stated in the text for acceptable sacrifices. Laws for sacrifice would have to wait until after the Exodus, thousands of years later. The situation is simple and unsophisticated. As a shepherd, Abel brought some lambs, and as a farmer, Cain brought some produce.

There is nothing wrong with the offerings. But there is something wrong with the offerer.

Inside view

'Then the Lord said to Cain, "Why are you angry? Why is your face downcast? If you do what is right, will you not be accepted"' (Gen. 4:6).

The reference to Cain's face is worthy of attention. What appears on Cain's face is a picture of what is going on inside him. 'Why is your face downcast? If you do what is right, will you not be accepted?' The Lord is saying to Cain, your inner attitudes make your worship unacceptable. This is the first step of Cain's folly.

He has fooled himself that the Lord does not see what is going on inside him. He hides his feelings. Later he'll try to hide his actions too.

- Do you recognise that God sees deep within you?
- Do you aim to hide your feelings of anger and bitterness without resolving them?

What is said in this part of Genesis provides an important lesson about the heart, the Bible's term for our inner attitudes and feelings. There can be no doubt that God sees within. As David put it to Solomon, 'The Lord searches every heart and understands every motive behind the thoughts' (1 Chron. 28:9). Jeremiah says, 'The heart is deceitful above all things and beyond cure' (Jer. 17:9). The effective cure comes only from God. The Lord says through Ezekiel, 'I will give you a new heart and put a new spirit in you. I will remove from you your heart of stone and give you a heart of flesh' (Ezek. 36:26).

The sin cycle

So what went wrong at the sacrifice? The answer is nothing. What went wrong happened a long time before the sacrificial offerings of Cain and Abel took place. What we see at the sacrifice is the unveiling of Cain's true character. He has clearly become bitter, angry and resentful over some long period of time. We don't know why. But the Lord warns him about nourishing the weaker aspects of his character. 'If you do not do what is right, sin is crouching at your door; it desires to have you, but you must master it' (Gen. 4:7). James expresses the same thought in the New Testament. 'Each one is tempted when, by his own evil desire, he is dragged away and enticed. Then after desire has conceived, it gives birth to sin; and sin, when it is full-grown, gives birth to death' (Jas. 1:14).

NEW ATTITUDES TO LEARN

That is sometimes known as the cycle of sin. First there is the emergence of wrong desires; then you let them gain a foothold; then a place of dominance; then finally the sin, the action, takes place. We are all made in the same way. And we all have to learn in God's strength to deal with our inner nature. That inner nature with its appetites and greed needs to be tamed. It provides us with temptations to indulge ourselves in all kinds of ways. We may lust after money, sex, power, or prestige. Our fallen inner nature is the source and battleground of all our struggles. The devil himself fights and contends with us on this pitch. This is where we must learn our discipline. In the strength of God, we must learn to extinguish and put to death what is potentially so destructive within us. 'The grace of God ... teaches us to say "No" to ungodliness and worldly passions, and to live self-controlled, upright and godly lives in this present age' (Tit. 2:11–12).

Yet it is remarkable how, like Cain, we can become anaesthetised to the dangers that lurk within. Without that insight, the erroneous thought emerges that the worship of God is a matter of externals. Like Cain, wrong motivations are ignored, with eventually disastrous consequences. But we cannot fool God. He looks on the heart. He knows our inner motivations. He knows the truth about us. Above all, he knows the depth of our helplessness, the extent of our pride, and the vehemence of our rebellion against him.

Shock treatment

'Now Cain said to his brother Abel, "Let's go out to the field." And while they were in the field, Cain attacked his brother Abel and killed him' (Gen. 4:8).

On Sunday morning, November 20th 1983, a small, close-knit community was at worship, in Mountain Lodge Pentecostal Church, in a little village called Kedy, in County Armagh, Northern Ireland, just close to the border. They were praising God together when suddenly, without any warning, the doors at the back of the church suddenly burst open. Two masked gunmen opened fire on the members of the church. Everybody dived for cover. Three died. Seven were injured.

The news of it shocked the world. It was so brazen, heartless and callous. Yet that was one of many thousands of shocking examples of unprovoked violence, which sadly happen all the time in different ways and in different places in the world.

The intention of the writer of this Genesis narrative is to shock his readers. He records a horrifying event with a special bluntness of style. His intention is anthropological. Look at what man can do! That is his message. There are no restraints. When there is real determination, nothing will restrain the worst dimensions of human nature. Nothing is sacred, not even worship, to the maliciously determined.

Just like us

The danger, when considering crimes against humanity, is to think that those who commit such offences are subhuman in some way, that terrorists, murderers and those like them are animals. But they are not: they are ordinary people, vicious, yes. It is an appalling thought to contemplate what they do, but they are not a race apart; they share our humanity and we need to learn from that. Look at what man can do! Where there is determination, nothing will restrain him.

So what is Genesis saying today about the crime of Cain? Its message is strong and thought-provoking. What does it say to normal, civilised, Christian-minded people?

The intention of the writer is to set us on guard. Consider the crime of Cain. Do not think any of us is *incapable* of such things. Cain was the first son of the parents of the whole human race. We share in his humanity. The depth of Cain's crime is linked with the depth of the fall. If you

NEW ATTITUDES TO LEARN

do not believe that you are capable of real destructive wickedness, you haven't yet understood the realism of the Bible's teaching about the nature of man.

Of course, there are some crimes against humanity which we *think* we can get away with.

- Destructive bitterness
- Anger
- Grudges
- Mental cruelty
- Hate
- Subtle expressions of revenge

All these are largely internal crimes. But aren't they of exactly the same nature as the crime of Cain? Remember Jesus's words: 'You have heard that it was said to the people long ago, "Do not murder, and anyone who murders will be subject to judgment." But I tell you that anyone who is angry with his brother will be subject to judgment' (Matt. 5:21).

It is the same point again. What happens on the outside is only the tip of the iceberg. Murder may be a dreadful thing, but the malaise sets in a long way farther back. And if we do not deal with the cycle of sin, with the bad habits of mind that cause us to court unforgiving attitudes, bitterness and grudges, who knows where they can lead when nourished by years of revengeful meditation and hate?

The mark of Cain

Cain imagined he could hide his thoughts from God. Now he thinks he can hide his deeds from him. 'The Lord said to Cain, "Where is your brother Abel?" "I don't know," he replied. "Am I my brother's keeper?"' (Gen. 4:9).

This is just an evasion. God knows what has happened. And the Lord announces his punishment. Cain is expelled from the land he has farmed. From now on he will be a wanderer. But here is the surprise. 'The Lord put a mark on Cain so that no-one who found him would kill him' (Gen. 4:15).

Nobody knows what that mark was, except that it stands for God's protection. It is a sign. Rather like a covenant sign. Like the rainbow after the flood, the sign of circumcision, or baptism. They all speak about God's agreement to keep his word of promise. And this is the surprise. Cain hit rock bottom. He was totally unruly within, in his inner self. It all spilled over, and this dreadful act of murder took place. Yet God offers him protection. This is a God who is prepared to be merciful to people who deserve no mercy.

Paradoxical

Human beings are an extraordinary paradox. We can do things of great beauty and of great ugliness. The story of Cain and Abel is not there to depress us. It is recorded for us to be realistic about our human plight. We share the humanity of Cain, and the humanity of IRA terrorists, as much as we share the humanity of a Mozart or Mother Teresa. So what should we make of all this?

- Recognise the depth of your need.

We all need to come to terms with what is going on inside us. Our wrong thoughts and destructive, jealous, angry attitudes need dealing with. They can end up tearing people apart in a sense as bad as any murder. And they will tear us apart in the process. Remember that Jesus put anger of this sort on the same level as murder itself.

NEW ATTITUDES TO LEARN

- Be clear about God's mercy.

A crack is opened up in Genesis 4 by the mark of Cain. We might expect extremely rough justice for Cain. But, in fact, he receives mercy. There's a punishment involved, but mercy is also in evidence.

Restoration and redemption

When we look at this from the perspective of the whole of the Bible, we know the mark of Cain is a foretaste of God's restoration plan for the whole human race. It tells us that our God is merciful. We know that for sure because Jesus Christ went to the cross so that our sins could be finally and completely dealt with. That means that nobody, however dreadful they may have been, is outside God's saving purposes. There's forgiveness and a new start for anyone who will turn back to God. All guilt is ended when Christ's forgiveness is received. We need no longer condemn ourselves or face condemnation from others.

- Do you need to seek that mercy and forgiveness from God. You don't have to have committed murder to be in rebellion against God. As we have seen, the problem goes deeper and is within. Remember the words of Jeremiah, 'The heart is deceitful above all things, and beyond cure.' The only cure is through the mercy we find in Jesus Christ.
- Be warned of the folly of Cain. You cannot hide your thoughts, nor your actions, from God. He knows you far too well for that.
- If you feel God is distant in some way, ask yourself if there is some area where you are still trying to uphold your own authority. In particular if there is a relationship where you insist on maintaining conflict by

your attitudes or actions. The Holy Spirit cannot inspire real assurance of God's love and forgiveness until you have forgiven others as you have been forgiven.

- Have you really turned your back on everything that is wrong? Or are you just sorry for the consequences? There is an important difference between repentance and remorse, of making a real break with what's wrong and just feeling sorry. Have you let old and destructive habits of mind, speech or behaviour persist unchecked? It's not enough just to *feel* sorry.
- Is there some sin which you are not prepared to face or to put right? Is there some wrong in your life which you are not really willing to give up? You need to face it. God loves you. He wants to help you. But he won't break through until you're prepared to face the issue and co-operate with him.
- Are you still nursing feelings of bitterness or resentment towards someone who has hurt or wronged you in some way? This is a major stumbling-block. Remember Jesus's words: 'If you forgive men when they sin against you, your Heavenly Father will also forgive you. But if you do not forgive men their sins, your Father will not forgive your sins.' It is meant to help us see the cancerous power of unforgiving attitudes.

New attitudes to learn

Unforgiving attitudes can wreck your mental health, certainly destroy your spiritual health, and badly upset and distort the lives of others.

- What action do you need to take on your negative attitudes to family, friends, neighbours and colleagues? Do you need to repent or apologise? Do you need to write a letter, make a phone call, or speak personally to someone today to sort out a problem between you?

NEW ATTITUDES TO LEARN 221

If you do, then don't delay. You must face up to it. We all have to learn to forgive and drop the charge, however badly we may feel we have been wronged. The need to forgive as we have been forgiven is right at the centre of Jesus's teaching. We all need to climb out of the habits of thought which we may have cherished for years but which nonetheless hurt and destroy our relationship with God and our relationships with others.

Facing conflict

In whatever way you are facing conflict in your life, will you aim to do all in your power to learn new inner attitudes which will make a real and decisive difference to the way you handle conflict? If you face up to this demanding task, it's true that you will not necessarily escape the storms of disagreement and differences of view you may normally encounter, but you will discover a new peace and liberty within which will help you circumnavigate the obstacles in your path.

From now on, then, though many conflicts can be upsetting and difficult, see if it is possible to regard such interactions with others in a positive, even optimistic way. Your changed reactions can make such a difference. Potential conflicts can become invitations for you to grow in a transformed humanness and overcome the destructive habits of mind, speech and behaviour, whose origins go back so many years in your experience.

You *can* change because the Holy Spirit brings you power to do so. Whatever you have learned from these pages, be courageous. Don't shirk the lessons. Aim to remind yourself of them regularly, and put them into practice. Don't let yourself be satisfied with your old half-hearted ways. Face up to your inner world and the part you play in conflict situations. You have new ways to respond, and new attitudes to learn. Let God be your strength as you aim to live a renewed and transformed lifestyle.

We all need to change and grow. Life doesn't stand still and nor should we. To be constantly adjusting to the daily challenges of the relationships in which we are involved is part of the call to wholeness and holiness which is both the challenge and the hallmark of the gospel. Whatever needs to change in your life *can* happen, as it is the supreme will of God that you should know his peace in all circumstances and situations. It takes energy and fortitude to face up to change. Whatever you may think or believe, you are no different from anybody else. Change is not beyond you for it is in the competence of God that it should happen. There can be no doubt. You will be helped the moment you decide that the work should begin.

Be encouraged, for the God of peace will be with you.

Christian Focus Publications publishes biblically-accurate books for adults and children. The books in the adult range are published in three imprints.

Christian Heritage contains classic writings from the past.

Christian Focus contains popular works including biographies, commentaries, doctrine, and Christian living.

Mentor focuses on books written at a level suitable for Bible College and seminary students, pastors, and others; the imprint includes commentaries, doctrinal studies, examination of current issues, and church history.

For a free catalogue of all our titles, please write to
Christian Focus Publications,
Geanies House, Fearn,
Ross-shire, IV20 1TW, Great Britain

For details of our titles visit us on our web site
http://www.christianfocus.com